More Praise for

A THOUSAND NAKED STRANGERS

"Action-packed . . . With blunt language and a raw narrative tone rich with gruesome detail, Hazzard immerses readers in the bloody, hardened reality of an emergency response team racing to accident scenes. . . . [Features] anecdotes both thrilling and startlingly gory . . . A vivid, pummeling ride-along with an emergency paramedic."

—*Kirkus Reviews*

"A well-crafted chronicle of gunshots, heart attacks, overdoses, and car crashes . . . Exciting reading."

—*San Antonio Express-News*

"An unstoppable adrenaline rush with lyrical moments of truth and beauty. Hazzard's unforgettable portraits of people in extremis, and the swaggering, sardonic, and ultimately courageous medics who take care of them, will stay with you long after you've turned the last page."

—Theresa Brown, author of *Critical Care: A New Nurse Faces Death, Life, and Everything in Between*

"Readers should fasten their seat belts for this wild ride with former paramedic Hazzard as he navigates Atlanta's seedier side while tending to a memorable—and gory—array of patients. . . . [His] unblinking view of chaos is not for weak stomachs, but it's variously raw, poetic, and profoundly hopeful."

—*Publishers Weekly*

"No one has a closer view into our fearful hearts than the paramedic, and no one writes it like Kevin Hazzard. He's given us a deep, intimate portrait of the toll it takes to, every day, witness our most vulnerable moments. Some nights it's the best job in the world, and some nights the worst, all in the same last breath."

—Joe Connelly, author of *Bringing Out the Dead*

"Fascinating reading."

—*People*

"Hazzard observes keenly, remembers faithfully, but also struggles to analyze his motives for loving those crazy nights on the bad side of town when the universe slips a gear and all hell breaks loose. *A Thousand Naked Strangers* is a brilliant delineation of what attracted him to the madness of his underpaid, underappreciated paramedical work and why it ended."

—J. Michael Lennon, author of the authorized biography *Norman Mailer: A Double Life*

"Hazzard excels at the small yet unforgettable details: what appears in the tread of his shoe, what scatters onto the floor of his ambulance. You'll begin this journey as a guilty voyeur, seeing things you really shouldn't, but, by the end, you'll be transformed into a respectful witness of a remarkable profession."

—Katrina Firlik, author of *Another Day in the Frontal Lobe: A Brain Surgeon Exposes Life on the Inside*

"It's Hazzard's insight into life's foibles and his skill as a writer that allow the reader to share his experiences and marvel at what often greets emergency medical technicians when they answer a call. . . . There's gore. . . . There's empathy. . . . There's even humor."

—*The Buffalo News*

"Gifted with a reporter's eye for detail and the wit and style of a bemused raconteur, Hazzard shows us what might happen if the medicos from *M*A*S*H* were miraculously deposited on the set of *Homicide: Life on the Street*."

—Bob Drury, coauthor of *The Heart of Everything That Is* and *Last Men Out*

"Get ready to feel the gunslinging, god-like power of running calls in the back of an ambulance. Here you'll learn what medics already know: along with the vibrators, maggots, crackheads, homeless shelters, and booby traps, it's the madness that both wrings you out and is the job's biggest turn-on."

—Julie Holland, MD, author of *Weekends at Bellevue: Nine Years on the Night Shift at the Psych ER*

"With an unsparing eye for all the details, Kevin Hazzard takes readers on a chaotic ride. . . . A gripping account . . . Hazzard is just the kind of human being you hope would come to your rescue."

—*BookPage*

"Reading this book is like watching *The Matrix*. Hazzard slows down the chaos and danger to allow himself (and the reader) to experience it. A paramedic's life is the closest thing to combat in the civilian world. To paraphrase a line in *The Bridges at Toko-Ri*, 'Where do we get these guys?' This book is one long rush."

—Phillip Jennings, author of *Nam-a-Rama* and *Goodbye Mexico*

"Hazzard has an eye for Atlanta's gritty detail—its true character and its true characters. Buckle up and prepare for an eye-opening plunge into barely controlled chaos."

—Judy Melinek, MD, coauthor (with T. J. Mitchell) of
*Working Stiff: Two Years, 262 Bodies, and
the Making of a Medical Examiner*

"Open Kevin Hazzard's excellent book and you might die laughing. You might also die of a broken heart. Or shock. Whatever, this writer will jolt you back to life with his sensational inside account of the world of emergency medical personnel. *A Thousand Naked Strangers* sends out a 911 call to readers . . . and those lucky enough to know these pages will never hear an ambulance siren the same way again."

—Charles McNair, author of *Land O'Goshen*
and *Pickett's Charge*

"A no-holds-barred look at what it's really like in the trenches. A paramedic's story of life and death and personal growth told from the back of an ambulance. Well worth the ride."

—Robert Lesslie, MD, author of *Miracles in the ER:
Extraordinary Stories from a Doctor's Journal*

A THOUSAND NAKED STRANGERS

A Paramedic's Wild Ride
to the Edge and Back

Kevin Hazzard

Scribner

New York   London   Toronto   Sydney   New Delhi

Scribner
An Imprint of Simon & Schuster, Inc.
1230 Avenue of the Americas
New York, NY 10020

Copyright © 2016 by Kevin Hazzard

First Scribner trade paperback edition September 2016

SCRIBNER and design are registered trademarks of The Gale Group, Inc.,
used under license by Simon & Schuster, Inc., the publisher of this work.

For information about special discounts for bulk purchases,
please contact Simon & Schuster Special Sales at 1-866-506-1949
or business@simonandschuster.com.

The Simon & Schuster Speakers Bureau can bring authors to your
live event. For more information or to book an event, contact the
Simon & Schuster Speakers Bureau at 1-866-248-3049 or visit
our website at www.simonspeakers.com.

Interior design by Akasha Archer

Manufactured in the United States of America

20 19 18 17 16 15

Library of Congress Cataloging-in-Publication Data is available.

ISBN 978-1-5011-1083-2
ISBN 978-1-5011-1086-3 (pbk)
ISBN 978-1-5011-1087-0 (ebook)

Some names and identifying characteristics have been changed.

You'll see some terrible stuff, I guess. That's how it goes. But try to look for the good things, too. They'll be there if you look.
—TIM O'BRIEN

The Menace is loose again . . . running fast and loud on the early morning freeway, low in the saddle, nobody smiles, jamming crazy through traffic and ninety miles an hour down the center stripe, missing by inches.
—HUNTER S. THOMPSON

Au revoir, gophèr.
—CARL SPACKLER, *CADDYSHACK*

Contents

BOOK THREE: TOP OF THE WORLD

BOOK FOUR: THE FALL

A THOUSAND
NAKED
STRANGERS

Prologue

I did nothing to save the first person who died in front of me. I simply stood watch and let her go. She was old and white and wasting away in a nursing home. Her death was unceremonious, but fast, and I was the only witness, earth's final sentry, there to do nothing but close the gates as she slipped through.

I was only twenty-six when she died, but already I'd squandered away two lives—the first as a failed salesman, the other as a reporter in exile. EMS was an accidental third act. It was early 2004, centuries ago. When I look back, I find it hard to believe this death and countless others happened, that at one time my sole purpose was to be present, as either anxious participant or indifferent witness. As with much of my EMS life, the memory is fuzzy: soft light filtered through gauze. It's only the details—the little ones that don't seem to matter at the time—that carry on. So really, what I have is more sensation than recollection, more feeling than anecdote.

This is how it all feels to me now.

It's my second night, and I'm partnered with a guy who never goes home. He's a firefighter in the next county, but he'll do anything for money and works a handful of part-time jobs. When he isn't here or at the fire station, he sweats over the fryer at

McDonald's. Just before ten, we're called to a nursing home for a sick woman. My partner is tired. He walks slowly, eyes to the floor, as we push the stretcher off the elevator and wander down the long corridor to the patient's room. We ease alongside her bed. A nurse hovers in the background, saying the woman didn't eat dinner, isn't acting like herself, and needs to be seen. I take her blood pressure, her pulse, count her breaths. Her eyes are closed; her skin—white and crinkled like parchment paper—is dry and hot. My partner asks for her papers. We don't ever leave a nursing home without papers. Most people in a nursing home can't talk, and those who can don't make sense, so even a question as straightforward as *Who are you?* doesn't yield usable results. So we get the papers, a thick manila envelope stuffed with everything from medical problems to next of kin. More important, it's in this packet that we'll find insurance information and whether or not there's a do-not-resuscitate order.

Ostensibly, we're here for the patient, but really all we care about is the DNR.

The DNR is the word of God Himself, written in triplicate and handed over not by Moses but by a big-boned woman in orthopedic nursing shoes. It's in these papers that we'll find answers to the uncomfortable questions that absolutely must be answered. What if she loses consciousness? What if she dies? Do I go all the way—CPR, electric shocks, slip a tube down her throat, drill a hole in her leg for medication? Or do I watch her swirl the drain until she disappears altogether? What does her family want? What would she want? The existence of this piece of paper, even its absence, means a lot. To everyone. At the hospital, the nurses will ask about it, and the doctors won't look at us until we've answered. At her age, in her condition, everyone will agree resuscitation, even if it could be accomplished, would be cruel. So does she have a DNR? The nurse says she does, that it's atop her packet, the first page in the stack. She leaves to get it.

And that's when it happens. Before my partner—who's leaning against the wall—coaxes his mass into action. Before I pull back the sheet. Before anyone addresses her directly. She opens her eyes—milky and unfocused—and tilts her head forward. Her lips part and then, without ceremony, she relaxes. Her last breath escapes. A single tear runs down her cheek.

I know instantly what's happened. But is it really that simple? That easy? The nurse has just said the patient has a DNR, so that drilled-into-my-head-during-school compulsion to act doesn't kick in. Instead, I spend the first few seconds staring into her vacant eyes, tracing the arc of that single tear—her final corporeal act—and marvel at this woman. Moments ago she was something to pity, bedridden and in a diaper. Now, plucked from her stained nightgown, she is cloaked in the wisdom of the ages. She knows why we're here and, more important, what's next. And if it's not the black nothingness we've feared all along, then how small we must look to her now. In dying she has crossed over. Or hasn't.

My partner, unaware she's dead, has finally come to life. He motions for me to grab the other end of the sheet so we can move her onto our stretcher. I need to tell him, let him decide what comes next, but I don't trust my own instincts. I'm brand-new at this, I've never watched someone die. My experience with the dead—recent or otherwise—is limited. If my partner doesn't notice, then perhaps she's not dead. The woman was hardly moving when we arrived and now looks no different. With a yank, we slide her over. He covers her with a sheet, buckles her in, starts pushing. I stare at her chest, her face, looking for signs of life that I know deep down I will not find. We grab her packet, and sure enough, the DNR is stapled to the top. We ride the elevator, step out into the cool night. With a sharp metallic click, the stretcher is snapped into the mount on the floor of the ambulance.

"I think she's dead," I say.

My partner stops and looks not at her but at me.

I clear my throat, tell him I don't think she's breathing.

He climbs into the ambulance, looks, feels, deflates. In the absence of the DNR, he might do something, but it's not absent. It's right there, and this document, drafted and signed with the sole intention of clarifying this woman's final moments, instead obscures our next move. Had she died in the nursing home, we'd leave her, but she's here now. Dead on our stretcher. In our ambulance.

We have drifted into murky water.

He calls the nursing home. "We're in the parking lot," he says. "Your patient is dead." "She's in your ambulance," the nurse tells him, "she's yours now." I stand outside while they argue. Our patient lies in state. What to do with her? The hospital doesn't take dead bodies, nor does the nursing home. This woman has died and no one wants her. She is a corpse in limbo. My partner hangs up. Fumes. He goes back in to explain, to plead, to threaten. I'm not sure why, but he leaves me in the back with her.

I sit in the ambulance and stare into the woman's half-open eyes. I grab the packet and flip through. If we are to keep each other company, I should at least know her name. Her birthday. Turns out she is eighty-eight.

There aren't many things you can do in the back of an ambulance with a dead woman. My cooler sits in the corner, but no. I could talk to her, but frankly, she is so recently dead, so unchanged from before, I feel as if addressing her directly will wake her. Well, not her but the ghost of her, which is worse. This may sound foolish, but I can assure you that all except the most gruesomely killed or severely decomposed look as if they'll sit up and begin talking at the slightest provocation.

I decide to call home. "Are you still awake?" I ask my wife.

She says she is. She broke down and started watching the latest episode of *The Sopranos* without me. "You're gonna love it." When I say nothing, she asks if I'm mad, and after a second I tell her where I am. Tell her that I'm alone with a woman I've watched die and who has become, thanks to my indecision, something of a refugee.

She asks how the woman died, and though I know this isn't what she means, I say, "Peacefully."

BOOK ONE

A Change of Plans

1

I've Made a Mistake

Six dead bodies. Each unknown to the others—different lives, different endings—stuck in six different morgues. Through the magic of photography, they've congregated here—naked, lascivious—in Appendix J of my EMT textbook. The first could be napping. The rest have been either burned or bludgeoned or shot in the face. One is a child. Though no longer alone, they remain nameless, remembered only for their usefulness to Western medicine. Their eyes have been blacked out, but all else is left uncovered. The woman has a huge mound of pubic hair: proof, according to the guy next to me, that she died in the 1970s. From behind us, a girl asks what page we're looking at, and the pubic hair expert—who hasn't yet gotten paid and so hasn't yet bought a textbook, who's leaning over my shoulder and breathing tobacco breath into my ear—tells her to flip to Appendix J. Page 310. He says he's seen plenty of dead people, and these, the ones in our book, they're nothing. The girl agrees. "You want dead bodies," she says, "good ones? Go to the Internet."

They're kindred spirits, these two, and they gravitate to each other, finally, thankfully, leaving me to my anxiety. I slam the book shut as tiny beads of sweat dot my forehead. I'm hot, dizzy, and my face is flushed. For a second I think I'm about to pass out, but then my mouth starts watering and I realize, no. I'm gonna puke. Swallow hard. A deep breath. Class hasn't started, the door is open. I can still leave without being noticed. Retreating? No, no, you got it all wrong. I am Richard Fucking Nixon, and this is peace with honor. Then the teacher walks in. The door shuts behind him. Eyes front, there is no escape.

He drops his bag on the table. Hands on his hips, legs spread wide. "Welcome to EMT school. Who's ready to get started?"

At the time of the 9/11 attacks, I was a reporter and my wife, Sabrina, whom I'd met in college, was working her way up in the world of ad sales. We lived in a small century-old bungalow on the south side of Atlanta, and everything was great until the world changed. In an instant we were at war. Since I'd graduated years before from The Citadel, many of my friends happened to be in the military. As I attended city council meetings and reported on budget cuts and judicial appointments, my friends were killing and being killed. Sabrina and I had dinner one night with a friend who led the first convoy of marines into Iraq. As he described the desert and the land mines and told stories of helicopters flying so low he could feel the heat coming off the rockets they fired, I thought of all the things I hadn't done.

I'd had my chances to join the military during college but hadn't. I thought about it again, but not seriously. Still, I wanted to be tested. I wanted to prove to myself that I could handle the pressure of life-and-death moments. How I'd do that, I couldn't say. Ultimately, opportunity would present itself in the form of a sewage disaster. The county was deep into an enormous waste-water project, and scaffolding leading down into the yawning tunnel collapsed one night. A half-dozen workers simply disappeared into the earth. My editor sent me to cover the rescue. I spent a long quiet night staring into the hole, hoping to see survivors but knowing there'd be only bodies. I wrote stories about the project, the faulty scaffolding, the dead. I wrote about the rescuers: specially trained fire-medics who carried themselves in a way that said they knew something, if not necessarily about the world, then surely about themselves.

In the summer of 2002, a tiny publisher put out my first book—a short and rambling coming-of-age novel. Once it was out, I quit reporting but stayed with the paper. Because I needed time but also money, I got a night job as a paper boy. In the span of two days, I went from writing newspapers to delivering them. Our friends thought I'd lost my mind. During the long dark nights, as I drove around delivering papers to the far reaches of Fulton County, my thoughts would wander to my friends in Iraq and Afghanistan. Slowly, those stories I'd written about paramedics crept back into my consciousness.

"So go back to school," Sabrina said one morning when I brought it up.

Shut up and take action—this is her solution to all problems. How nice it must feel to be a type A in a world gone soft. That afternoon I started poking around on the Internet, and by night-fall, almost by accident, I was enrolled in an EMT program at a local technical college.

This was a rash decision. I knew nothing about medicine, and the only experience I'd had dealing with emergencies did not end well. It was the summer of 1997, and I was leading Jet Ski tours when two guys crashed into each other. I didn't see it, but I heard the thud, and when I got there I found them floating in the water—one startled, the other missing a mouth. His eyes were wide and bulging. His face below the cheekbones was gone; blood and teeth dripped into the water. His skin hung slack where his jaw should've been. I was young, scared, overwhelmed. I did the only thing bystanders are asked not to do in an emergency: I panicked.

Seven years later, here I am. In EMT school. The door is shut, class has started. I'm embarking on a career that will require me not merely to witness emergencies but to participate in the rescue. I can't help thinking I've made a huge mistake.

With me in the classroom are two dozen misfits, all looking for a respectable job. Our instructor is Alan, a lifelong medic who came up when EMS was in its infancy. He tells stories of running calls on dark streets and in cramped apartments. His tales smell of blood and desperation. They're real and exciting but scary, since eventually the dying patients will be ours. And though we're a long way from that, the photographs in the book make clear what awaits us. Maybe he can read my mind—hell, maybe I'm not the only one having second thoughts—because Alan tells us, right out of the gate, if we're not sure we can handle this, now is the time to leave. A couple of people laugh as though the mere suggestion is ridiculous, but I'm not one of them. I didn't grow up wanting to be an EMT, nor do I know if I'll like it. What I do know is I want to get hip-deep in the things that matter. I want to know if I'm more than the kid who panicked that summer day in 1997. I want to know if I can be counted on.

So I stay.

2

From Zero to Hero

Modern medicine is practiced in the light. It is technology and advanced diagnostics, a digital brain whirring at fiber-optic speed. It is ultrasounds and sonograms and blood work and radiation, human intelligence blown up and expanded to realize inhuman capabilities. Patients are treated in a controlled, sterile environment where accountability, procedures, protocol, and hierarchy are all carved in stone.

Precise, clean, cerebral.

EMS is none of these things.

According to Alan, EMS is wild and imperfect. Just like our patients, it's dangerous and a little mad and possibly contagious. Alan regards the job as a throwback to nineteenth-century house-call medicine—patients don't come to us, he says, we go to them, and where and how we find them, well, that, too, is part of the story. Once in the field, we should expect no help; we'll have no team of lab techs waiting for tissue samples or blood samples or stool samples. We'll have a blood pressure cuff and a stethoscope. A wristwatch. A flashlight. We'll have common sense and eight months of school. Alan promises that once we're done with class, we'll find EMS simple and uncluttered and intensely personal, because it's one thing for a patient to die on a hospital bed beneath the glare of a thousand watts of fluorescent lighting, but it's something else entirely for a man to die on his living room floor with his family looking on. And yet Alan believes the essence of EMS is not that a man has died here in so intimate and messy a setting. The essence of EMS is that we know we'll be back tomorrow, because even from here—surrounded by the hysteria of an unexpected death—we'll hear a baby coughing in the next room.

To be good, Alan says, we can't just treat patients; we must study them. Learn their language, their habits, their streets and houses, their peculiar beliefs, fears, and failings. Many of these people will be nothing like we are, nothing like anything we've ever seen. Of course, he says, there are the sane, the stable, the middle class, and the wealthy—the boring—who sometimes call, but in the upside-down world of EMS, these are the lunatic fringe. The heavy lifting is done by people who call every day, for every conceivable reason. Invited as we are into their disparate lives, we'll not only treat them, save them, and pronounce them dead; we'll also learn from them.

Alan reviews the syllabus and I drift off, start writing in my textbook. I think about what he's said and, daydreaming, imagine myself stumbling on some alien culture, removed from mine by time and space. I think of all the artifacts I'll find, how I'll carefully unearth and catalog them. How I'll set them aside for later viewing in the museum of my own recollection.

In the margin of my textbook, I write, *EMS is medicine as modern anthropology.* I stare at it for a bit, then circle back and add a question mark.

"All right," Alan yells. "Let's take a break."

• • •

Our class begins in March and wraps in December, putting the education of an EMT—one of two people sent to save your life should the worst happen—at eight months. Our school amounts to nothing more than a certificate program and doesn't count toward any college degree, associate or otherwise. That first night I buy a hardback textbook and its accompanying workbook, which neatly organize the course material into sections—medical emergencies (all of them), trauma (a rainbow of injuries both accidental and intentional), CPR certification, and a federal course on the toxic material sloshing around in the back of semi trucks.

Alan opens by explaining exactly what it is we, as EMTs, will do. We'll bandage, we'll splint, we'll immobilize suspected spinal fractures. We'll start IVs and give oxygen and ventilate anyone not breathing. Over the next few months, he says, we'll learn the Heimlich and get CPR-certified. He'll show us how to drive the ambulance, when to use the lights and sirens, how to navigate around other cars and—when they crash—how to cut them open with the Jaws of Life. Alan explains that an EMT is the junior member on the ambulance, the understudy, hands operating at the behest of the paramedic's brain. Medics—as paramedics are known by everyone in the field—undergo an additional eighteen months of training. They dispense a long list of drugs for a dizzying array of complaints. They are trained to read twelve-lead EKGs, detailed tracings of a heart's electrical activity. Should a patient stop breathing, the medic will intubate: the art of slipping a breathing tube through the vocal cords and into the trachea. It's a medic who uses the infamous paddles to shock a heart back to life.

Alan says that either the EMT or the medic can drive, but if the patient is sick and needs critical treatment, the medic will be the one in the back rendering care. If you have a serious medical emergency, the medic will help you. If things are bad enough, and sometimes they are, the face of a medic may well be the last thing you see.

Every medic was once an EMT, and nearly every EMT will eventually go back to school and become a medic. Though lifelong EMTs exist, they're a rare breed—by upgrading to para-medic, an EMT can increase his pay by as much as ten dollars an hour. Alan tells us that in some states, two EMTs will work on an ambulance—known as basic life support—but in Georgia, all 911 ambulances are advanced life support, meaning they carry at least one medic. For budgetary reasons, few services staff double-medic ambulances. But Alan assures us that we won't merely be low-paid underlings. EMTs exist, he says, to serve as a safety switch. They function as roaming eyeballs, their minds uncluttered by drug doses and defibrillator settings; they can see the simple explana-tion for what seems complicated. "So pay attention," he says. "This isn't just your job. It's also your legal obligation."

Turns out, until we finish school, we're still innocent by-standers, and should we harm someone in a rescue attempt, we'll be protected from litigation by Good Samaritan laws. But once we finish and become official EMTs, we'll not only be fair game in a civil suit, we'll be required to save any and all lives in need of saving. Whether we're on duty or not.

When he tells us to open our books to chapter one, the only sound is the soft whoosh of pages turning.

During our first break, I meet a guy named Brian who's been working at a motorcycle repair shop. He's bored and looking for something new, and being an EMT or a firefighter or, frankly, anything sounds better. Brian chain-smokes, and I crack jokes, and little by little we attract a couple of others until we've assembled what will be our group for the duration of the course. Aside from Brian and me, our gang includes Justin, a former high school baseball star; Randy, a thick, surly redneck bursting at the seams who burns off excess energy by racing on the dirt-track circuit; and Tim, a part-time mailman who doesn't look a day over fourteen.

None of us has a particularly compelling reason to be here other than the vague and difficult-to-describe notion that perhaps, maybe, this will be a cool job. That's probably not what Alan wants to hear, but as I'll learn, it's not uncommon. For all the talk of heroes and sacrifice and selfless service, EMS is just another job. There are, to be sure, people among us who grew up wanting to save lives, but many more enter the profession as capriciously as we did. Disturbing as it may be, the raw truth is that often enough, the people showing up to your medical emergency do so because this was the only respectable job they could get with a GED and a clean driving record.

For the first few weeks, the mood is light, but eventually a disquieting reality takes hold. We'll soon enter the world of EMS and be expected to perform in an environment of intense pressure. Some of us, owing to how the percentages inevitably work out, won't live up to the moment. I'm suddenly no longer the *only* one with doubts. It's clear in our faces, in the looks I get from other students—always accompanied by a nervous laugh— that say, *Yeah, I heard the lecture and memorized the words, but will I remember them later, when I'm with a patient?*

Me, I feel less sure of the answer every day.

Three nights a week I drive the forty minutes to class, sit at my little desk, open my book, and listen. The lectures veer wildly from topic to topic, and after a few months I feel no more prepared to handle emergencies than on my first night. The way I calm my nerves is to remind myself that this is a nationally recognized curriculum. If I study and memorize and pass, then when I get hired, I'll be no worse than anyone else fresh out of school. I'll be exactly where I'm supposed to be. It's this thought, this little cocoon of denial, that carries me through the self-doubt.

Then one night the cocoon bursts.

It happens during our first break. We stand, stretch, wander outside, and collect into little groups. My four friends and I are standing in the evening sun just beyond the door when Justin, the former ballplayer, says he has a friend in EMT school across town. They started a week after us, but they're already doing scenarios. Every day. We all freeze. Scenarios are hypothetical emergency situations devised to put to practical use what we've learned in the classroom. Their purpose is to get us accustomed to bringing the knowledge in our heads down to our hands, which is the only place it matters. Because all of an EMT program's students are untrained and inexperienced, scenarios are the key qualifying step.

Alan told us we'd be doing them at some point, but he never said when. I'm not sure we've learned enough practical information to devise scenarios, let alone work our way through them. We've discussed a lot of things in general but almost nothing specifically. There were the two weeks dedicated to anatomy and physiology, but they felt more like a dead sprint than anything else. We learned about kinematics—the study of how force acts on the body—as a means of anticipating the different injuries in someone who's been hurt in a rollover versus a head-on collision. But what those injuries look like, how to spot them, and what to do about them, we haven't gotten to *any* of it. That's cause for concern.

It's not that Alan is a poor instructor. He's just easily distracted. Tucked away in our corner and whispering, we come to the conclusion that the problem isn't Alan. It's our classmates. The class has formed two cliques, the four of us and everyone else. Those not in our group seem more interested in smoke breaks and war stories than learning, and in our opinion, they're holding us back. Not that our gang is necessarily any smarter. Hell, two days ago Alan pulled Randy aside and told him the only way he'd be allowed to finish the course was if he promised never to work in EMS. But we're behind, and not only are those outside our group unconcerned, their grab-assing is part of the problem.

From that night on, every time the lecture strays from the practical, every time someone derails Alan with stupid questions, every time the class ends without the passing on of real and usable knowledge, the ticking clock that's been present since day one gets louder and louder until it's no longer a clock but a freight train, steel wheels screaming as it barrels down the tracks.

"I have a quick question. If you have a second," I say to Alan one night.

Alan nods as he tucks his books into his backpack. He's the training officer for a local fire department, and teaching is his second job. The minute class is over, he just wants to go home. I inch to the left a few feet—if he's going to slip out, he'll have to run me over to do it.

"Are we behind?"

Alan hefts his bag, slips the strap over his shoulder, and starts to walk before he realizes I'm blocking his escape.

"On the material, I mean."

He shakes his head. "Nope."

Oh.

He tries to get around me. I shift my weight.

"Because we're entering month three, and we haven't done any scenarios yet. Are we supposed to be doing those?"

"We haven't done scenarios?"

"No."

"Yeah, we did a few right after we talked about ongoing assessments."

"We haven't learned those."

"We haven't?"

"No. Only initial assessments."

Alan leans right, lets his bag rest on the desk. "Shit. And we're entering month two, aren't we?"

"Month *three*."

"Month three?"

Now I'm alarmed. I feel the rattle and hum of the freight train, its horn drowning out the world.

Alan looks straight at me. "Shit."

"You already said that."

He does the math in his head, nods, then lifts the bag back onto his shoulder. "Wednesday," he says. "Get here early. We have some catching up to do."

3

Dead Mannequins

Wednesday passes in a blur. So do Friday, the following Monday, and every day after that. I take my book everywhere, reading then reciting the telltale signs and symptoms of impending death, matching each to its corresponding course of treatment. The nearly dead are never far. I am strange company in the waiting room.

This level of immersion creates an immediacy that borders on paranoia, on obsession. *Am I actually learning from all these flash cards, do I need to make more, who knew there were so many ways to stop bleeding?* It's all so new, so foreign, so much like that period of childhood—first or second grade, maybe—when you're old enough to know you're alive and one day will die, yet young enough to still believe that a thin vein of magic runs just beneath the surface. Everything crackles with the electric charge of wonder.

We spend half of every class studying the list of life threats EMS is equipped and trained to handle. Seizures, asthma attacks, acute problems associated with congestive heart failure, fast heart rates, slow heart rates, no heart rates, orthopedic trauma, burns, penetrating wounds, low blood pressure, high blood pressure, broken femurs, broken necks, even broken minds. We sit and listen. After an hour we push the tables aside, break out the expired drugs, and get down to the serious business of saving lives.

"Hey, ma'am," I say, nervously reciting the script to the mannequin at my feet. "What seems to be the problem today?"

"BAM! You're dead. I just shot you in the head," Alan crows, curling his fingers into a gun and pulling the trigger. "And your partner? He stepped on a downed power line near the ambulance. He's sizzling. Can you smell it? I can smell it. Who else can smell it?"

Alan is a born taskmaster—imperious, impatient, demanding perfection. And no form of imperfection aggravates him more than scene safety. The safety of you and your partner, he says over and over, is paramount. "A dying patient becomes a dead patient if you're careless, like Mr. Hazzard here. Now," he yells, "start over. Do it *right*."

I'm standing in front of the class, hands in my pockets, eyes locked on the mannequin. On a table is a blue jump bag, a huge canvas duffel carrying every piece of equipment an EMT is allowed to use. I'll have to correctly use all of it before I can sit. Alan faces me in a chair, legs crossed. He repeats the dispatch: person down, problem unknown.

My voice always sounds weak and far off when I do these. "First thing," I say, "is scene safety."

"Louder," Alan yells. "The people in back can't hear you. If they can't hear you in a quiet room, how will your partner hear you when the cops start shooting up your scene?"

I take a deep breath, then rattle off all the potential hazards waiting to do us harm—an active fire, speeding cars, collapsing

structures, angry bystanders, angry dogs, even angry patients. I
contracted leprosy during my first scenario, so I pantomime putting on gloves. Once Alan is satisfied, I shift my attention to the
patient. In reality, the patient is always the same—a naked and
discolored mannequin missing his left leg—but for purposes of
this class, it could be anyone, man, woman, or child. Sometimes
the patient can talk, other times we get information from a bystander. Often the patient is unconscious, occasionally he doesn't
speak English.

We ask questions: What's your name? . . . What's the problem? . . . Can you breathe? Alan provides answers: John, I think
he's dead, *dónde está la biblioteca*. But it's not enough for us to
know what questions to ask and what the answers mean. We
must prioritize them by what will kill the patient first. Start with
the airway, move to breathing, then worry about circulation. In
that order. Even if my patient's guts are tumbling out, I have to
make sure he has an open and clear airway and he's adequately
breathing before I can worry that he's been disemboweled.

Tonight I quickly move through the early stages of the scenario without finding any problems. So far so good, but this is
where it gets tricky. Were this patient actually a patient and not
merely a dummy, the problem would probably be obvious. But
it *is* a dummy, and I'm standing in front of my class. Alan taps
his watch. Tick-tock, tick-tock. I launch into a battery of questions: What have you been doing, are we inside or outside, do I
notice anything strange?

Alan sits up. "Where?"

"On, uh, on . . . her skin?"

"Bingo. She's got a rash on her foot, spreading up her leg. In
fact, now you notice an EpiPen on the table."

"Is she allergic to anything?"

"Yes!" Alan yells, ecstatic. "She is. But before she can say to what, she collapses."

I quickly recheck that her airway is open, and for not immediately panicking, I'm rewarded with the following: "Outside the window, you see a lawn mower surrounded by a cloud of angry bees." *Allergic reaction.* I launch into the treatment of anaphylaxis—at least, the portions of the treatment an EMT can provide. The studying, the notecards, they're paying off. For me, at least. Despite my near-perfect assessment and my early and aggressive intervention, the patient dies.

Alan tells me not to worry about it. This is medicine, not TV. Sometimes mannequins die.

4

Living and Breathing Dead People

It doesn't even occur to us that we haven't placed our partially trained hands on an actual human until Alan walks in and tapes three pieces of paper to the chalkboard. "Sign-up sheets," he says. "Time for your ride-alongs."

We're five months in at this point, three months until we finish the course. After the course, we'll take the National Registry exam. Passing it allows a person to work as an EMT anywhere in America. But before we get to all that, we have to do our ride-alongs. A ride-along is exactly what it sounds like: a daylong apprenticeship in the back of an ambulance, shadowing medics and EMTs. Someone asks what service we'll be riding with.

You can hear a pin drop when Alan says Grady.

Grady Memorial Hospital looms large in Atlanta's consciousness. To many, it's a place of horror stories and ghost stories, of lawless halls teeming with the poor, the crazy, and the critically ill. My first close view of it comes in the dark of a June morning as I await the start of a four A.M. ride-along. The giant lighted cross atop the hospital glows red in the dark sky, and steam from a pair of smokestacks slowly rolls out like a blanket of fog. There is a large moon in the otherwise empty sky. Somewhere in the distance, a lonely siren wails.

I'm here early, and there's nothing to do but wait. I pace, I overthink, I worry—about what I'll see, what I'll be asked to do, how I'll respond. I wonder what these guys will think of me. Grady EMS is the 911 provider for the city of Atlanta. The phones ring off the hook, and Grady medics are busy to the point of exhaustion. They're broken in, tested, and competent. They're the standard by which all medics around Atlanta are measured. They prowl the city's worst streets, wander housing projects at night, and frequent jails and crack motels. Years of working in these conditions have taught them to sniff out the signs of illicit drug use and recognize when a situation is about to go wrong, almost instinctively. Grady medics are experts in treating their patients, calming their patients, and occasionally fighting their patients. They're cocky and untucked and stand in stark contrast to their spit-polished but rusty counterparts in the fire department.

I'm brand-new and all but useless. I feel nothing but intimidation.

Finally, two Grady medics emerge from the shadows in cobbled-together uniforms—more utilitarian than official, more mercenary than medic. They nod and tell me to get in, and before I know it, before I'm ready, I'm sitting in the back of an ambulance rumbling through the heart of a sleeping city.

All ambulances carry the same smell, a dizzying cocktail of disinfectant, plastic, and diesel fuel mingled with scents leaking in from the outside world. But there's something else, a smell you can't quite put your finger on and which, in truth, doesn't exist. It comes not from any physical source but from the knowledge that people have sweated, bled, and died in here. The fact that so much has happened in so small a space will immediately dispel the notion that those who die in violent or sudden circumstances forever haunt the site of their demise. An ambulance, at its most spacious, is a five-by-ten rolling memorial to the abruptly and tragically dead. How many have slipped away in any one of them is simply unknowable, and yet not one story exists of lonely and angry specters whispering threats to frightened paramedics.

My rumpled preceptors wear all this death with style. The job has changed a good deal over the years, and the two guys I'm paired with, Pike and Wooten, came up in the brawling Wild West days when Atlanta was the murder capital and surviving the daily parade of shootings and stabbings required a hard-bitten and ruthless approach. Pike is wiry, rangy, with a thick goatee straight out of the Civil War; he chain-smokes and pounds coffee with the manic energy of a guy who never sleeps. Wooten is silent and bitter, his thickness a testament to the poor diet so common among public safety workers. While Wooten sits silently in the passenger seat, Pike drives like a madman, talking without stop, without prompting. "This whole area, everything you see," he says, waving his arm indiscriminately at all we pass, "is a fucking shithole."

The shithole he's referring to is an area known locally as the Bluff—five square miles of drug houses, flophouses, abandoned buildings, squatters, drugs, violence, desperation, and the constant *woop-woop* of sirens. The Bluff is Atlanta's answer to Compton, to Chicago's South Side, and to the Heartland's countless and nameless meth-riddled trailer parks. It is where all of Atlanta's heroin is sold and most of its crack is consumed. People here live in aging projects or derelict bungalows; when they aren't getting into trouble, Pike says, they're calling 911. He stomps on the gas and tears open the air with a long, loud burst of siren.

Wake up, motherfuckers!

My father-in-law spent a year of his life in Vietnam, an experience that affected him deeply and about which he's generally tight-lipped. There are some topics, however, he *is* willing to discuss, one of them being the futile efforts of the 1960s-era army to prepare its conscripts for jungle warfare. For instance, he loves to tell how he trained with an M14, never even laying hands on an M16—the weapon with which he was expected to fight and win a war—until after he was already in Southeast Asia. And he'll laugh as he describes the World War II–style combat tactics taught to him by his drill instructors, men who'd never seen a jungle and who never once addressed the unique difficulties and strategies of jungle warfare. All of the skills he eventually acquired for keeping himself alive came from war-weary nineteen-year-old kids who'd gotten there a week before he did.

EMS training is not nearly as inadequate, but the very nature of practicing medicine in streets, bathrooms, living rooms, elevators, construction sites—literally anywhere—renders obsolete many of the rigid procedures drilled into our heads during school. And so Pike is standing next to the ambulance, a cigarette dangling from his lips, rattling off a list of techniques I've learned in school that aren't only poorly suited for the streets but could, in some cases, get me or my partner hurt.

"Backboarding," he says. "Do it like they show you, straps running crosswise over their body? Fuckers'll slide right out."

"Slide out?"

"What happens when you got 'em strapped like that and you try carrying them down stairs?"

"They slide out?"

"They fucking slide out." He takes a heavy drag, followed by a languorous exhale. "Run those straps between their legs," he says, "and crisscross them over their chest. Fuckers aren't going anywhere."

On and on it goes.

"Now, when it comes to fighting patients—"

"Wait, what?"

"What?"

"Fighting? You said fighting?"

He laughs. "You think all these fuckers are glad to see you? That they're gonna hop on out to the ambulance for a quiet ride to the hospital?"

I ask why anyone—especially a person who presumably has called for my help—would attack me just for showing up. Pike shakes his head as though I'm almost too dumb to help, then ticks off a list that includes seizure patients, drug overdoses, violent psychs, drunks, head injuries, pissed-off family members, and those who, for no good reason, are simply pissed off at the world and to whom I represent a great place to start exacting revenge. "It's all how I approach them," Pike says, "the way I assert my authority." He goes on to describe a tricky blend of rigidity and leniency—where he draws the line and what he does the moment they cross it—that determines the direction these calls will take.

"Handle it right and you'll be fine. Fuck it up and you're in for a long afternoon," he says. He grabs a pack of patient restraints and asks if I know the proper way to restrain a patient. I don't, but before he can show me, we catch our first call.

For the next few hours, I watch Pike and Wooten run calls from the close and inescapable confines of an ambulance. I'm mesmerized. We run calls in projects and high-rises and on the litter-strewn shoulder of I-85. We pick up a child with a fever, drop off a woman with abdominal pain, and bandage a man who's been sliced open by his girlfriend during a domestic dispute. There is a fluidity to these medics' movements that borders on grace. I don't see how I could ever be this good.

Around midafternoon it finally gets quiet. There's no scheduled downtime in EMS, no lunch hour, no bathroom breaks, no nothing, and when it's busy, you just run. So you eat what you can, when you can. That afternoon we eat greasy chicken from a dirty fast-food restaurant, then fall into a stupor. I'm just starting to drift off to sleep when the ambulance starts moving. We've got another call.

I haven't yet shaken off the fog of grease when the ambulance jerks to a halt and, for the first time all day, I hear Wooten's voice: "Holy fucking shit."

Strange things happen in this world. One of them happens today. A man none of us knows and whom we'll never see again spent all last night bingeing on a strange mixture of cocaine and heroin known as a speedball—one drug to cut the trail for you, another to send you down it. Heroin, being what it is, calms while the cocaine fuels. The problem is that the heroin has a shorter life span than the cocaine, and so, out of nowhere, that smooth high suddenly becomes all sweat and frustration and grinding teeth. After his buzz turned sour, our patient spent the afternoon homicidally racing his car through the streets. Eventually he lost control, sped down a ravine, and smashed into a tree. The impact broke both legs, but he's too strung out to notice. Confused and combative, he simply hopped out and took off running—and the broken bone ends immediately poked through his skin. By the time we arrive, the damage is so extensive that the upper and lower sections are jutting out in a grotesque sort of crisscross pattern.

For the first time all day, Pike is quiet. Wooten suggests perhaps we should get out. I stand next to them in front of the ambulance—heart pounding, pupils dilated—partially horrified, partially hypnotized, and totally unsure what to do. Once Pike has drawn up a sedative, we approach the patient like zookeepers sneaking up on an unruly bear. Our quarry sees us, hesitates, and squares his shoulders. Pike and Wooten recognize what's about to happen. I do not.

They jump out of the way. I'm frozen. The patient—wild eyes, hulking mass, broken and scissoring leg bones—charges me. I never even react. Just before he plows me over, Wooten, more agile than his body bloat suggests, leaps out and knocks him down. Pike piles on top. I watch as the three of them roll around until Pike screams out in pain, whales the guy with a wild elbow, and yells for me to grab the needle. Somewhere in the tussle, he dropped the sedative, and it's now out of his reach. This snaps me out of my daze. I grab the syringe, pop off the top, and jab it into the man's ass.

Then I back up. Pike and Wooten slowly untangle themselves and watch as the drugs work their magic. The man rolls onto his back, twitches, and starts snoring. Pike grabs the stretcher, and the three of us snatch him up and load him into the ambulance.

Once the doors are closed, Pike and Wooten laugh and exchange the weary glance—part exasperation, part celebration—that always passes between partners after the dust settles and you find yourselves sweating and exhausted but alive and in one piece. Wooten takes out a pair of scissors and cuts off the guy's pants. Pike and I set to work on tying restraints.

My crash course on tying someone's hands and feet to a stretcher with soft restraints is contained in a single sentence: The legs should be spread wide and tied at the ankles; left arm is down at the side; right arm is up by the ear. Careful consideration should be given to the knot itself. Pike assumes I'm good with knots. That assumption is incorrect.

We're only a few minutes down the road when our patient begins to stir. Sure, he's been sedated, but there's still all that cocaine. His eyes open. He twitches, jerks—a wild animal caught in a snare. He turns to me and shakes his head in fury, then flops back, sits up, kicks his legs, and blows out a lungful of hot anger. He pulls against the restraints. His right hand, the one Pike tied to the stretcher near his right ear, doesn't budge. But the left hand? The one I tied? It's already coming loose. He runs his fingers over the shoelace-style knot and smiles. Or maybe not, it's hard to tell through my rising panic. Either way, he yanks on the knot and his hand is free. Just like that, he's up. Wooten throws a sheet over the patient's face and holds him down. I reach for his free arm but miss. A paralyzing pain shoots through me.

Dude has grabbed my nuts.

I try to endure the pain, swat away his hand, and regain control of the situation. Instead I let out a scream that is terrified and desperate and too high-pitched to be mine. Pike stops the ambulance. He jumps in the back, and together he and Wooten properly restrain the patient. The transport continues, though I hardly notice. There is nothing but the pain, the echo of my long humiliating scream, and a quiet period of huddled convalescence.

At some point we drop the patient off, then run more calls. The day ends. I go home, and whatever I tell Sabrina or my classmates of that first day is edited for content. There are other ride-alongs, more classroom hours. There are other things I do right, other moments I live up to. But as always, lessons are drawn from mistakes, not victories.

So I learn that knots are knots, that patients will turn on you, and that what happens in the ambulance—well, it's best that it stay there.

5

Failure Is an Option

Unlike the first four months, the second half of my EMT course speeds by. We attend class, do our ride-alongs, and work shifts at a local hospital. All this is background noise; nothing matters anymore except the impending doom of the National Registry exam. Alan devotes a chunk of every class to the exam—passing along his tips and warning us not to panic, not to let Registry become a huge stumbling block.

National Registry consists of two parts—the written and the practical—and sports a fail rate somewhere near 50 percent. Everyone is anxious. If I don't pass, I can't work. It's that simple. If I choke, I'm just a paperboy who took an EMT course. Alan assures us that we can retest but only so many times—after that, it's back to school. I silently voice to myself the things I must remember: *Know the material, trust your instincts, avoid the fatal mistakes—scene safety, scene safety, scene safety.* We study. We prepare. We wait.

Our course work ends in mid-December. After eight months, it's strange to be set free from the three-nights-a-week mooring we've relied on for so long. School, even technical school, becomes an end in itself. On the last night we do a few scenarios, and then Alan asks if we have any final questions. Not one hand goes up. We're simply ready to leave. After class I head to a Mexican restaurant with my little group of five. We drink, we laugh, we reminisce about this strange bubble we've been living in for the last eight months. Nothing about tonight feels final until the tab is paid and we're drifting out the door one by one. Life is a series of cycles—each nothing but new people, new memories, and eventually, a new ending.

That weekend Justin and I drive to Savannah to take our exam. We don't leave much time to spare on the drive down, and rather abruptly, we go from sitting in the car to sitting in a medical annex building, staring at a test booklet. I finish in an hour, and even as I'm walking out, I can't remember a single question. We have dinner, sleep, wake up, and take our practical exam.

In contrast to the written, the practical portion is agonizingly slow. There are five stations and a hundred testers. We sit for hours in a stuffy room waiting our turn. Finally, everyone cycles through and it's over. We line up outside a door and enter the room one by one to see who passed and who failed. More waiting, more waiting, holy fuck, the waiting. Justin goes in first. He emerges shaking his head—he's failed and will have to retest. Things have just gotten real. I go next, close the door, and smile at the five assembled faces. Someone asks my name. He shuffles through a stack of papers and nods. "You pass. Congratulations."

That night I throw away my books and get drunk.

Two days later, Sabrina and I are in Paris. We've each been here before, though separately, and all the sightseeing that must be done has been done. We wander the Latin Quarter eating gyros and sandwiches. We walk the Seine at night and eat Nutella-and-banana crepes under the Eiffel Tower. We drink wine all day and ride the Metro drunk just to listen to the gypsies play the accordion. At midnight on New Year's Eve, we're under the Arc de Triomphe. It's nothing but a celebration until 12:01, when the city shuts down the entire party and forces hundreds of thousands of people from the Champs-Élysées. We're drunk and cold and have nowhere to go. The night quickly devolves into a riot. We ring in the New Year cloaked in a rolling fog of tear gas.

Two weeks later, we return home to a stack of mail. Buried ten envelopes deep is a letter from the National Registry of EMTs. I have my numbers. I'm officially an EMT.

6

A Job at Last

Midnight. Early February 2004. Atlanta has frozen over, and the gravel parking lot surrounding FirstMed Ambulance is buried in frost. I'm half-asleep in the back of an ambulance. My partner and her girlfriend are drinking Malibu rum in the warm comfort of the office. Just a few months ago, when I was in school, I pictured this EMT gig going differently. I expected dedicated and earnest medics crowded around a dying patient, all of them pounding futilely on his chest while telling him he's not gonna die, not on their watch.

This is not that kind of place.

How I landed here, at FirstMed, is the punch line to a joke I'm not ready to laugh at. I text Sabrina—which is awkward because my fingers are numb—and tell her this isn't what I signed on for. In all caps, I type I AM DONE. She texts back. Says I signed on for the weird. This is weird.

I stuff the phone in my pocket, pull the blanket over my head, and swear to myself I'll quit in the morning. Just as I'm starting to drift off, the front door opens. I bolt upright. As in most FirstMed ambulances, the dome light doesn't work, so I can't see what's happening in the cab. I hear someone rifling through the glove box, the ashtray, the console. I'm waiting to hear the engine rattle to life when the side door flies open and we're eye to eye—me on the stretcher with a blanket, he wearing two pairs of pants and a ripped pink jacket. He has one black eye, a few cracked teeth, and a wild beard braided just below the chin and strung with plastic beads. His hands are cracked and caked with grime, and he has plastic shopping bags tied around his shoes. He's half-drunk and fully homeless and takes me for a fellow traveler. After saluting my savvy sleeping choice and apologizing for waking me, he grabs a blanket and disappears into the night.

Where he came from and what his story is, I can't say. But my story—the one about how I graduated at the top of my EMT class and still wound up here, in this ambulance? Yeah, I know that one.

As soon as I passed the EMT exam, I quit delivering papers. After nearly a year of working late nights, seven days a week, it was good to be gone. I woke up the next morning and set about finding employment. I had high hopes, and why not? This was medicine, a field everyone will tell you is always hiring and has limitless possibilities, a career field where no two days are the same.

My first call was to Grady EMS. They said no, told me I needed experience, and suggested I try the fire department. So I did. I contacted every department in the area and was told by every receptionist in every municipality that they hired once a year and then only through a meandering process of forms and test dates and agonized waiting. The only remaining option if I wanted to run 911 calls was Rural/Metro Ambulance, which covered the parts of Fulton County not handled by Grady. I lived in Fulton, I wanted to work 911, and this would help me get a job with Grady. It seemed like the perfect fit. I called. A woman answered and told me they'd just hired a bunch of people the day before but not to worry because they'd be hiring again soon. How soon? Six months. I told her I didn't have six months. She paused, then: "Maybe you should try the fire department."

I left the house. This wasn't how it was supposed to go. I'd quit my job, delivered newspapers, attended EMT school, passed an exam administered by a nationally accredited organization. All for nothing. I was unemployed and out of options. I stopped at a red light, closed my eyes, and rested my head against the wheel. Just as the car behind me started to honk, a beat-up ambulance breezed by. I flipped on my blinker. I had no idea where it was going but figured if I followed until it got there, then . . . What I'd do at that point was unclear, but what choice did I have?

Following the ambulance wasn't easy. After all, there were speed limits, traffic lights, stop signs, not to mention crosswalks and pedestrians, all things I had to navigate. Not the ambulance. It wasn't using the lights or sirens, clearly had no emergency to handle—the driver was simply indifferent to local traffic laws, maybe to all laws. I was sold.

A few quick turns and I found myself in another world. This was a new place, a new city, nothing but abandoned lots, strip clubs, burned-out buildings, shady car dealerships, and scrap yards hemmed in by corrugated steel walls. Weeds grew through the sidewalks until, without warning, the sidewalks ended. We drove on. More liquor stores, more pedestrians, more beat-up cars. A handful of run-down houses, the lawns nothing but clay littered with broken plastic chairs and children's toys. And then, without turning on a blinker, without braking, the ambulance yanked a hard right and skidded to a halt in a gravel parking lot. I rolled by as slowly as I could. The sign above the front door said FirstMed Ambulance. The place looked near death, as though the building, the ambulances, the employees, everything needed to be put down. I pulled a U-turn and whipped into the lot.

The front door was the flimsy sort you usually find on a cabin or an outhouse and squeaked so loudly that everyone inside turned and looked as I walked in. The place was all cigarette smoke and daytime television. I was in shorts and flip-flops. Perhaps I'd acted a little hastily. A woman probably a decade younger than she looked peered at me from the other side of a long cigarette. She asked what I wanted. I shrugged. A job? A minute later, I was sitting in a small office with a giant man named Don. Don, too, was smoking when he handed me a single sheet of paper.

"Just write your name, phone number, address. All that stuff," Don said as he crushed out one cigarette and lit another. "Do you, uh, do you have numbers?"

"Phone numbers?"

"EMT. You *have* passed Registry, right?"

I told Don I had passed Registry, though it wasn't until later that I realized, oddly, not passing wasn't a deal-breaker. Don simply nodded and talked about everything, *everything*, except the job. His love of sci-fi novels, his decade-old divorce to a woman he still lived with, and the recent household addition of his neighbor and her three young sons. When I finished filling out the application, he took the paper and tossed it atop a towering stack of folders and notebooks made more unstable by the occasional crumpled paperback.

"Welcome aboard," Don said, making it clear that this single sheet of paper represented not only proof of my credentials but also a formal job offer and my acceptance thereof. Any questions?

Yes. In fact, I had tons. What job did I just accept, and when did it start? What did it pay? Was I supposed to wear something other than shorts and flip-flops? Don nodded and lit another cigarette. Some people loved this place, he said. There were employees who'd been there for a decade. Some didn't last a week. He himself had been at FirstMed twenty years, during which time he'd been fired and rehired, by his own conservative estimate, thirty times. Hours were flexible; so was dress. "Something that looks legit" was all he said regarding uniform. First-Med also had the contract for the Georgia Dome, which meant I could volunteer to work Falcons games and sit on the sidelines.

It all sounded good. Then, checking to see that the door was shut, Don told me not to listen to the rumors. The accusations of Medicare fraud were a line of shit. FirstMed had been investigated multiple times, he said proudly, and each time the investigators came up short of having enough evidence to prosecute. *Maybe,* I thought, *this is my signal to run.* Job interviews aren't supposed to include assurances that your new employer, despite the rumors, despite nearly all the evidence, is not actively engaged in insurance fraud—as far as the government can prove.

But Don seemed nice, and I'd been offered a job. He asked if I could come in tomorrow. I said yes. What time should I show up?

He shrugged. "I don't know. Eight?"

7

First Day

At ten minutes to eight, I yank open the door and step into a haze of smoke. Sherry—parked in the same spot as yesterday, probably smoking the same cigarette—nods. Without taking her eyes off the TV, she motions to a neatly stacked pile of equipment.

"You're in 304," she says, turning the TV up a notch. "Jonathan will be here eventually."

I wander outside and look for 304, the ambulance that will carry me to my first patient, the ambulance in which I might actually save a life. In my mind, 304 is muscled and gleaming, smelling of disinfectant, a fully stocked diesel-powered extension of the modern emergency room. In reality, 304 is a piece of shit. It's unwashed and dented to hell. The antenna's broken, the tires are bald, and there's a piece of cardboard taped to the back window that reads TAG APPLIED FOR. I toss in the gear and look around. The upholstery is torn and stained—*stained*? Stained. My mind quickly moves beyond 304's aesthetics, its disrepair, its jagged corners—bristling with tetanus—to the terrifying reality that today I'm not here merely to watch and learn. I'm here to work. I look around, and it's all so foreign—the wall-mounted suction unit, airway devices, bandaging supplies, long backboards, traction splints, and rubber bag for ventilating patients called a BVM—all of which I've been trained and signed off on but little of which I really know how to use. All the lessons from class—the acronyms, abbreviations, anecdotes, body parts—are running confused and frantic circles around my mind. I close my eyes, press my hands together, and say out loud, "Please God, let Jonathan know what he's doing."

On cue, the side door flings open and Jonathan jumps in.

"Morning. I'm—"

"Go fuck yourself."

I freeze, hand extended and wavering in the air. Without looking at me, Jonathan tosses a bag on an empty shelf and drops into the captain's chair. It's then that I see the Bluetooth earpiece. Relieved, I wave. He doesn't acknowledge me.

"Yeah. That's what I told him," he barks into the air. "I mean, seriously. This is what it's come to? I gotta go to work and come home to my apartment, to accusations of fucking other guys? In our bed? And what did I do? I'll tell you. Not a fucking thing. Keep this up, though? I'll fuck every guy I see."

Jonathan looks at me.

I blink away the sweat.

"I gotta go," he says.

He hangs up. I hold my breath. Jonathan is a light-skinned black guy, easily six-four, probably 230. Every time he shifts his weight, the entire ambulance rocks with him. "We got everything?"

"Well, I grabbed what Sherry told me to get, but I'm not sure if it's everything. This is my fir—"

"Good. Let's get breakfast. I'm starving."

• • •

A long line of eggs crackles on the griddle at Waffle House. Jonathan dumps sugar into his coffee. He dips his spoon in, stirs, nods to me. "You work yesterday?"

"Actually, this is my first day."

"Off all weekend, huh?"

"No. First day first day."

"Oh. Cool. How long you been doing this?"

"First day first day. First day."

He stops stirring. Regards me closely for the first time. "Like your first day on an ambulance? As in never worked before? Ever?"

"Yup."

"Why didn't you say something?"

His demeanor changes and suddenly he is talkative, smiling. He grabs his phone and calls the office, tells Sherry I'm a baby EMT, fresh out of the package. Give us any call that comes in. When the food comes, he talks with his mouth full. He claims, improbably, to be a med school dropout, a former cop, and an ex–marine reservist. EMS is the only thing that ever really suited him, he says, so here he is. He smiles. "Job sinks down into your bones," he says. "You'll see."

I ask him what exactly it is that FirstMed does, and he explains there are two types of ambulances. Obviously there are the 911 ambulances, but there are also the others: private ambulances whose sole purpose is to take the infirm to and from appointments. That's us. To work for a private service is to spend your professional life wandering through dialysis clinics and nursing homes, neither of which is pleasant. Dialysis clinics are sterile white rooms filled with the tang of bleach and the soft whirring of machines that slowly drain your blood like calibrated vampires so it can be scrubbed and then pumped back in.

Nursing homes are nursing homes—slow death in an industrial setting. I ask him why we have so much equipment if all we do is take patients to appointments, and he explains that dialysis is complicated and taxing on the body. Sometimes those patients simply die.

But there's something else, too, which is that nursing homes sometimes fudge their math. Think of it this way, Jonathan says. A nursing home patient slips and falls. If the staff calls 911, this suggests an emergency—something, anything, they can't handle on their own, which raises questions they'd rather not answer. If they call a private service, a non-emergency service, it suggests a small but concerning problem, something caught and handled early. He shoves food in his mouth and says: It's sleight of hand, but it works. And it happens every day.

I clear my throat. "Don said something about insurance fraud?"

He waves his empty cup at the waitress and smiles. He explains it like this: "We charge more for transporting a patient in an ambulance—one who can't sit up or who needs the special care of EMS during transport. And so long as we can prove the necessity for an ambulance and not, say, a much cheaper wheelchair van, Medicare will pay the higher cost." He stabs his fork into a pile of hash browns. "So, we simply document the medical necessity of transporting the patient by ambulance. Sometimes it's true and sometimes . . ." He laughs. "You're new," he says. "Trust me. You're gonna see all kinds of things."

Our Nextel chirps and he grabs it. "Yeah?"

Sherry's voice crackles over the diner. "Got one for you."

• • •

Crestview Nursing Home is perched atop a sloping hill and rises from the clay like a tombstone memorializing its uncounted and uncountable dead. To the east lies a forgotten cemetery where, during the 1996 Olympics, police found several murdered hookers but not their killer. To the west its neighbors are a strip club and an abandoned apartment complex, remembered—by those who remember it at all—as the spot where a toddler was killed by a stray bullet that passed through his bedroom wall. To the rear sits a long brick building that is rumored to have served as a dormitory for chain gangs working in South Atlanta. Other than that, there is the highway and nothing else.

Crestview is monstrous. How many thousands have slowly slipped down the drain of life with bellies full of Crestview Jell-O is impossible to say. Most of the home's residents live and die anonymously; they are the toothless faces of Georgia's poor and infirm.

Jonathan and I step off the elevator. I'm immediately assaulted by the air, heavy with the stink of dirty diapers, reheated food, and unwashed bodies. We squeeze around a resident who stares but doesn't move. He's nothing but an open mouth, a vacant face. A geriatric still life in dirty pajamas. Down the hall, it only gets worse. Fish-eyed men in bathrobes stand frozen in corners; legless women roll around in squeaky wheelchairs. At every turn, more appear. The blind, deaf, demented, and forgotten shuffle toward us with pained yet purposeful movement, propelled, zombie-like, by the scent of real-life humans.

We press on toward the nursing station and find the place in total chaos. Files teetering on top of food trays, threatening to topple over. Nurses, a half-dozen, at least, cackle in the island dialect found in nearly all of Atlanta's long-term care facilities.

Somewhere—be it Jamaica, Barbados, the Dominican Republic, or Trinidad—someone is recruiting nurses, tons of them, making it hard to find a single nursing home not echoing with the distinctively lyrical and unrushed accent.

Of course, they ignore us. Jonathan casually reaches for a file marked 22b and asks what the problem is. The nurses stop talking, annoyed by the intrusion. Without turning toward us, one of them says, "It's rum nine, bid twennnty-twooo-bee. Din't eat nooo breakfuss this marnin'."

They continue on with their conversation. Jonathan interrupts them again. "That normal?"

"Wit youuuu tink?"

"Don't know. Don't know him. Or is it a she?"

We obviously aren't going to take the patient and disappear. The nurse sighs and snatches the chart. We follow her to room nine, where she stops at the foot of bed 22b and starts thumbing through the paperwork. The man in the bed, Mr. Perry, does not look good, even to my untrained eyes. His black skin is shiny and packed tight like spoiled sausage, swollen to the point of bursting. His dry lips are cracked, eyes yellow and sunken, breathing heavy and fast. He's so febrile that I can feel the heat rising from the bed. His limbs are shriveled and contracted, his belly bloated as if he's swallowed a frozen turkey. A feeding tube pokes out of his gut just below his ribs and runs to a bag of the brown liquidy stuff eaten by people on feeding tubes.

Jonathan points at the line. "So, if he's on a feeding tube, how did he not eat breakfast? Because it seems to me all you'd have to do to get him to eat breakfast is turn it on. Did you forget to turn it on?"

The nurse thrusts the chart toward him. "Din't you reed dis?"

"Nope."

"Line is clogged. No floooow."

"I see."

"And hee's gut a feeeever."

"For how long?"

"Staaaarted las' night. Night staff don't tell us nutin'."

Jonathan and the nurse stare at each other. There's no way that his fever, his distended abdomen, his clogged feeding tube, or even his dirty diaper are new as of the last twelve hours, but there are some things not worth arguing over. We take Mr. Perry and his chart and leave. Outside, it's like we've been released from prison. Or a coffin. We wheel him to the ambulance and load the stretcher. As I climb in to get a set of vital signs, the doors slam shut behind me. I freeze.

Certainly Jonathan isn't going to leave me, an EMT with under two hours of experience, alone in the back of an ambulance with a man whose list of complicating medical factors exceeds my own medical vocabulary. Certainly this is a joke. Then I hear the front door open, and the ambulance sways under Jonathan's weight. The engine fires up. I poke my head through the window connecting the front of the ambulance to the back. "What the fuck are you doing?"

Jonathan smiles. "Going to the hospital. Don't worry. You'll be fine."

"I'm not worried about me. I'm worried about him."

"He'll be fine. Or not. Dude's literally on his deathbed. What's the worst thing you could possibly do?"

I look at Mr. Perry, a feverish, bloated, heavy-breathing bag of slowly dying humanity. "You gotta get back here. Seriously."

The ambulance starts to move.

"This isn't funny, Jonathan. It's incredibly far from funny."

"You're right. This isn't funny. This is your job."

I grab the blood pressure cuff and check Mr. Perry's pressure. If he has one, I can't tell what it is. I've pushed my fingers into his neck to count his thready pulse when, without warning, he opens his mouth and shoots a geyser of dark brown blood straight up into the air.

I scream for help, but Jonathan keeps driving. There's nothing to do but roll Mr. Perry onto his side and let him soak the cabinets, the equipment, the sheets, everything, with partially digested blood. A Stephen King novel has nothing on this. I am scared and furious, and even after we get to the hospital, I ignore Jonathan. When we've dropped the patient off, Jonathan shakes his head as he surveys the damage in the ambulance. "This is gonna be an expensive cleanup."

Five minutes later, we're standing behind FirstMed's ramshackle offices, haggling for a better price. Jonathan has ten dollars in his hand. Richard, a local homeless guy, shakes his head.

"Come on," Jonathan says. "It's a pretty straightforward job. All I have is this ten-dollar bill."

"That's not a ten," Richard says. "That's a bunch of ones."

"Ten ones. Same fucking thing." Jonathan slaps the bills against his hand. "So?"

To my astonishment, Richard hops in and starts cleaning. Without so much as a pair of gloves. He hoses out the back, disinfects the ceiling, stretcher, and floor, then replaces all the dirtied items from the cabinets. Jonathan sits back, pointing out little gobs of blood Richard has left behind. "Missed a spot right there, man. No. There. Under the seat."

When Richard's done, he hops out, snatches the stack of

ones, and shambles off. "Call me any time," he yells as he disappears into the liquor store. "Any time."

And none of this is an aberration. Everything I've seen since laying eyes on a FirstMed ambulance has been perfectly normal to everyone around me. Nobody finds it strange that I was hired without providing any proof that I'm an actual EMT. Though we are ostensibly an ambulance service, no one cares that people occasionally drink on the job. When I tell people about Jonathan's stunt with Richard, everyone keeps waiting for the twist that justifies my revulsion. But no twist ever comes. The revulsion is mine alone.

The place is a misfit circus, a sort of way station for EMS cast-offs. It's owned and operated by an incredibly kind couple about whom it is hard to say anything negative. At one time or another, nearly every medic and EMT in Atlanta has worked at FirstMed. Anyone in need of extra cash, who's been fired, or who is fresh out of jail or rehab can walk through FirstMed's squeaky front door and find a spot on an ambulance. Or a place to live.

I quickly learn that Richard isn't merely one of the homeless men wandering the streets but that he lives, quite happily, in an abandoned tractor-trailer behind the FirstMed office. He runs an extension cord from the offices to the truck, which he uses to power a fan, a lamp, a hot plate, and a thirteen-inch black-and-white TV. Then you have Mike and Linda. Mike is a skinny white guy with stringy hair; Linda is a skinny black woman with stringy hair; neither looks even slightly trustworthy. Mike is an occasional crack addict who was fired for his addiction, and Linda is a dispatcher who was fired for being Mike's dealer. In the span of a single week, each shows up—clean and sober—and is greeted with open arms. "Give it a month," Jonathan whispers. "They'll be back at it."

One night a medic named Lyle—tall with a shaved head and the droopy-eyed look of a man who knows it's his lot in life to be perpetually on the clock—disappears with an ambulance. Nobody notices he's gone until the cops call to say they've caught him getting a ten-dollar blow job from a man wearing high heels. The manager bails him out but insists Lyle do the disinfecting himself.

Did I say the place is a circus?

Sabrina is standing at the open driver's door, shaking her head. "I can't drive an ambulance."

Jonathan is undeterred. "Of course you can. Just put it in gear and drive."

"No," Sabrina says. "I mean I can't. It's illegal."

"So?"

Sabrina looks at me. I tell her it's a bad idea but not the worst idea. I'm wrong, of course, but if you spend enough time around lunatics, their normal slowly becomes your normal.

Two minutes later, we're rumbling down the road. It's a slow Saturday, and Sabrina thought she was just meeting us for lunch. Now this. It doesn't seem so bad until Jonathan flips the sirens on. Sabrina's head snaps over. "What are you doing?"

"Just drive."

"I can't. Not like this. Turn those off."

"Too late. Drive."

So she drives. An ambulance. With the lights on. Down a crowded city street. She isn't supposed to be here, not in the back, not anywhere. And yet here she is. Driving. She runs a few lights and eventually makes her way back to the car. She's a little shaken but giggling, and when I ask if she liked it, she nods and says, "I kinda did."

In May I finally escape. I'm standing outside a dialysis clinic, there to pick up yet another legless patient and carry her back to yet another run-down nursing home, when my phone rings. It's the recruiter from Rural/Metro, the company with Fulton County's 911 contract. My heart pounds as she tells me they're about to start a new-hire class. "Are you interested?"

"Very."

"Can you start next week?"

"I can start right now."

She laughs and then launches into a disclaimer: The opening is in South Fulton County. North Fulton, she says, is much more popular because it's affluent and safe and people don't call as often for toothaches and headaches and babies with a fever. South Fulton, by contrast, is all run-down apartments and poverty and roach-infested ghetto.

She pauses, clearly expecting me to hang up. And then, with hope in her voice, she asks, "Are you ready for this?"

BOOK TWO

Fresh Meat

8

Pray for Carnage

Picture a lawn mower blade. Heavy and dulled by the constant thwack of sticks and rocks. Rusted steel and motor oil covered in a fuzzy green layer of minced grass. It spins on a bent axis, the bolt loose and the blade wobbling ever so slightly as it goes. It's early morning, the grass wet with dew. A foot slips and disappears under the mower's bruised metal frame. The blade, more belligerent than precise, hacks through leather, rubber, and cotton, right on down to sweaty black flesh and crooked bones. A single scream rises in the air, joining the pungent cloud of oil smoke from the two-stroke engine. The mower stops. Three toes, starting with the big one and working inward, are hacked off and scattered in the grass. Never to be found, just gone.

"Gone. Sheeeit." Our patient looks at me, his pained expression replaced for a moment by a horrible realization—his toes are gone. He'll never walk right, never run. Never go barefoot. He shakes his head. "Sheeit." He's sweating on the stretcher, shedding diced-up bits of grass. He smells like blood and gasoline. "Sheeit."

This is my first call at Rural/Metro, my first call on a 911 ambulance, and I'm happy. Glad to be here, to be the one to catch this call, glad he cut his toes off. Somewhere there's a doctor who'll tell him there's nothing to be done, that she can sew him up but the toes are a memory. "Get a cane," she'll say. These words will break his heart but not his spirit, and he'll get over it and get better—eventually, he'll get back to work. But I'm not here for the diagnosis or the cure. I'm here for the blurry and frantic moments right after the injury. My partner, a medic named Jerry, has been around a few years, so a man with three missing toes barely commands his attention. But me? On my first day? It's magic. We drop him off and run more calls.

We end the shift with a woman who's spent the night in the company of a dozen steak knives and an ever growing puddle of congealed blood. Jerry and I wander the house, collecting knives and looking for the second victim—no one has this much blood. But it's just our patient and her demons, and though she won't tell us what she's done, she says it's bad, too bad to tell anyone, and that she just wishes she could die. There's a cleaver on the kitchen floor, bloody and rusted. Next to it sits a bent knife, the skinny kind used to filet fish. She kicks it dismissively, derisively, says it's useless. No good for cutting through human flesh at all.

These are the endcaps to my first day, and when it's over, I don't want to leave. All I can think about when I get home is the start of the next shift. All I want to do is run calls, treat patients, drive the ambulance, stand in line at a convenience store in a rough part of town. This uniform, a light blue shirt with patches on the arms, opens doors. It conveys knowledge. The feeling is electric, being an insider, knowing that should anything happen, I'll be the one called out to fix it. Every word the radio breathes into the stale air of the station sets me on fire. EMS is the greatest show I've ever seen, except it's not a show, it's all real. No, it's more than that—it's reality distilled and boiled down to its essence. It's life and (hopefully) death, and unlike the general public, I'm invited and allowed to wander freely amid the debris. So send me *anything*. I'm on a 911 ambulance. I'll run whatever you've got.

9

Killers

Within a month Jerry has been fired. I walk into the station one morning to be confronted by two supervisors and the director of operations. They sit me down, say they need to ask a few questions. Someone asks if I want anything, and out of sheer panic, I say that water would be nice. The director of operations is short and bald, fat on an epic scale. We're in the bunk room and the fan is off. He's starting to sweat. From the next room we can hear ice plinking into a glass, the tap running. When the water comes, I drink half the glass.

I wonder why two supervisors and the director have come this far, why they didn't just fire me by phone. Maybe there's a chance I can talk my way out of this, whatever it is. Hell, I haven't been here long enough to do anything right, let alone something that'll get me fired. As for Jerry, well, he probably deserved to get fired. He has a shitty attitude toward patients, toward our supervisors, toward the job in general. How and why he got into EMS, I don't know, but he stayed too long. Every medic in the county knows it. Even I know it. And that's saying something. These last few weeks have been so disorienting, I hardly know my own name. It's been all I can do to keep from drowning.

Scarcely a minute has passed during which I haven't learned something new, something that could theoretically make the difference in someone else's life. How to talk on the radio, talk to a doctor, talk to patients. How to do all the things I learned in school—size up a scene, backboard, dress a wound—not just properly but quickly. How to start IVs in a moving ambulance, how to start them on the old, the sick, the injured, the nearly dead, even the clinically dead. I have no experience with any of this, so for the first few shifts, whatever Jerry says, I do. However, it quickly becomes clear that Jerry has lost his way.

As the crew of a 911 ambulance in Fulton County, we have a simple mandate: Transport everyone who calls. Whatever the reason. We can't say no. If they call, they get a ride. The woman who calls at three in the morning because she's had a nightmare? Transport. Toothache? Transport. The guy with back pain who's clearly faking and just needs a ride downtown? Transport. But Jerry doesn't transport. Not these people and, if he can help it, not anybody. One night we run a stabbing outside a nightclub. The place is going nuts like Mardi Gras in a strip mall. Two girls—dressed to party and drunk on cheap liquor—start fighting. Someone breaks a beer bottle and stabs our patient in the neck. It's not a throat-slashing kind of thing, but the wound is nasty, like raw hamburger, and after I bandage it, I tell the girl she needs to come with us. But she's not having it. She has no time for us, no time for a tetanus shot, no time for stitches, and certainly no time for the hospital. Before I can launch into all the reasons she needs to go, Jerry tells her if she starts walking away, we have no right to chase her down. We'll simply let her go. No hospital. No bill. No questions.

When I bring it up later, Jerry brushes me off. He says it's her choice, and who are we to tell her what to do? Seems to me we're precisely the people to tell her what to do, but he rolls over and goes to sleep.

This is the story I'm waiting to tell the director and the supervisors, the one I assume they've all shown up to hear. Instead, the director says, "Tell me about his girlfriend."

"This is about *her*?"

Jerry is dating a medic from Alabama, and he's been trying to convince her to come work with us. One day I show up at work and she's here in full uniform. Jerry says she's going to ride with us, see if she likes it. He's vague on whether this has been approved. I figure she'll ride for a few hours, then take off. But she never takes off; she stays the entire shift. That night she crawls into Jerry's twin bed in our little bunk room. The noises I hear after the lights are out—kissing, giggling, zippers and grunts and the gentle sway of a shitty mattress—are noises lonely people pay for. But I'm not lonely.

The director runs a meaty palm across his forehead and wipes the sweat on his pants leg. He says the ride-along was never approved, that he can't begin to imagine why Jerry would think he could just bring someone to work. "There are rules for a reason," he says. "Valid reasons, safety reasons. You understand that, right? Say you understand it."

What I want to say is *Look, I was just following Jerry's lead, and Jerry, well, he's one of those people who does what he wants*. But unlike Jerry, I want to keep my job.

"Yes, sir. I understand."

And really, I do. For an entire day, a medic who never applied to Rural/Metro, who was never interviewed, whose credentials were never verified, and who was never hired, rode an ambulance and treated patients. Clearly, this sort of thing can't happen.

My ignorance saves me from being fired but not from getting chewed out. The director says I should've known better, should've asked, should've told somebody. He's sitting on Jerry's bed, and as he talks, it groans under his weight. The old familiar creak. I ask myself: *If I tell him about that night, about what happened on that mattress, will he see the humor?* Finally, he struggles to his feet—one final squeal from the overburdened mattress—and says, "Long story short, Jerry's gone. We'll get you a new partner."

What I get is not a new partner but a parade of part-timers. They all ask what happened to Jerry, and when I tell them, they're not surprised. They nod, say they saw it coming. Maybe not the exact means of his undoing but something. People like Jerry, with a shitty attitude, they're common in EMS. To a person, each part-timer insists burnout is rampant. The long days and longer nights, the missed holidays, the missed birthdays, it all starts to add up. I am, my partners constantly remind me, simply an EMT, and that means I'm making eleven dollars an hour—about what people make at Starbucks. How many baristas are bled on or puked on or asked to save a life?

I'm told everyone gets burned out. That if I stick with this long enough, I'll burn out, be born anew, and burn out again. Most people eventually move on, though a few stay forever. Most who stay love it. But there are others—the ones who are here and wish they weren't, who are either too lazy or too lost to find something else. These people, like Jerry, become Killers.

Though I've seen Jerry in action and I know what to look for, these temporary partners, they're not satisfied. It's not enough to have seen it in Jerry, they say. I need to know the signs so I can spot the transformation years from now, either in another partner or, God forbid, in myself.

My education takes the form of late-night horror stories, the accumulated knowledge of an entire career distilled to its antithesis—here, then, is what a medic shall *not* be. I hear a thousand of these stories, all the careless, lazy, even mean things Killers have done. In the end, only one stands out. Like a good jab, the story is short and to the point and leaves you wondering what else might be out there.

An old man is found down, barely breathing and on the verge of death. He has cancer. He has heart failure, lung failure, kidney failure. He has no family and even less hope, and the medic who arrives at his house simply places a gloved hand over the patient's mouth.

There are stories and then there are *stories*. Maybe that's all this one is. Maybe not. I'm not certain Jerry would've gone that far off the rails, but thanks to his girlfriend—with her easy-to-open Velcro fly and that squeaky twin bed—I'll never have to find out.

10

Tourists

I'm getting better every day. Learning if still green. I'm not yet good—that comes with time—but I'm getting there. I'm told repeatedly that the way to learn is to keep my eyes open and my mouth shut. Just listen and absorb. Which is easy, because I listen to everything they say, *they* being my rotating cast of irregulars. As a group, they're better than Jerry but far from promotable. That's not to say they don't want to be here, just that they're here for reasons entirely their own. They're Tourists, and filtered through their strange and slightly out-of-focus perspective, that they're here for all the other things this job allows them to do—that for them practicing medicine is secondary—makes perfect sense.

My most frequent part-timer is Josh, a body builder with enormous teeth, big white monsters spread wide enough to walk through, and a body to match: six and a half feet tall, chest like a beer keg, shoulders wide as a doorway, a booming voice cradled in a South Georgia accent. His shirts look to be about my size, tattoo-tight and rolled up at the biceps. He is one of the nicest guys I've ever met—always smiling, always laughing—which I suppose is your prerogative when you're big enough to rip the arms off a bear. He's been a medic twenty years, and while he has the skills to walk through any emergency with the aloof grace and silent speed of a Siamese cat, his specialty is old women.

They call every day for every reason imaginable, and his approach is always the same. There she is—nothing but bones inside a nightgown—and in he walks, subtle as a bull elephant. When he reaches her, he sits, regardless of where she is—the bed, the floor, naked in a half-filled bathtub—and he takes her little bird hand and talks as if the only reason he's shown up is to have a casual conversation. In his own way, he has a genius for it, although his mind is somewhere else.

In between calls, he devotes his full attention to bodybuilding magazines. He isn't just reading. There's something almost religious in the way he studies them, a thick finger marking off each word. Occasionally, he slaps the pages and flips back to cross-reference what he's just read with an article from the day before. He keeps the magazines stacked in a duffel bag, and at the start of each shift, he removes them with great reverence, not merely a subscriber but a holy warrior sitting down to pray the knowledge into his head. He reads for hours, consumed and silent until, without warning, he lurches out of his seat and crashes down next to me. He jabs a big sausage finger at the page and discusses whatever has caught his attention—how the heavy use of diuretics really cuts up your calf muscles, or the comparative benefits of various pre-competition body oils, or the superior aesthetics of a brown sun-given tan versus the orange hue of a tanning bed.

He carries another duffel bag dedicated solely to nutrition. Three times a shift, he yanks back the zipper and pulls out a blender, a big spoon, a huge plastic cup, and an enormous tub of whatever protein shake he's taking this week. In goes the water, followed by two or three heaping scoops of white powder, a sprinkle of creatine or androstenedione, and then he claps on the top and mashes the puree button. He always offers me a cup, and when I say no, he gazes at me—just a poor, hopeless civilian—as if all I need is the right combination of baby oil, sunburn, and muscle shake to turn things around.

He's here because our schedule of one day on and two days off allows him time to train. Plus, there is the stress of being up all night, running around in the heat, the constant activity. He needs this lifestyle—along with the diuretics—to get lean, because tough as he is, he's powerless when it comes to food. He confesses that when he doesn't have a show coming up, his willpower gives out. "For lunch alone," he tells me, "I'll eat a rack of ribs, three hamburgers, a couple pounds of fruit, and a block of cheese." One night he devours an entire bag of jumbo marshmallows on the way to the hospital.

The body builder is memorable, but he's not alone. There is Jose, also a Tourist, though much quieter and a man who takes a while to open up. When he does, it's early evening, the sun setting behind a derelict apartment complex near the Atlanta airport. Planes rumble overhead. We're standing over the bloated body of a man who, judging by the smell, was shot a few days ago. There's nothing to do but wait. Wait for the medical examiner. Wait to make sure some kid doesn't stumble on him. Wait for the body to burst. Finally, after twenty minutes, Jose starts talking.

"I always drive with my window down," he says, smiling. "If it's hot, cold, raining, doesn't matter. Fucking snowing. I always keep it open. It's because of this." He tugs at the collar of his uniform shirt. "Girls love this shit."

The girls, the ones who get excited by uniforms—who are

drawn to them, who can't resist—proposition him. In Walmart, at McDonald's, at the gas station. While he's transporting a patient. "Last girl pulled up while I'm at a red light and shouts, 'I've never been fucked in the back of an amba-lance before.'" Jose shakes his head. "That's freaky, right? People die back there. Love me a freak, though."

Jose admits EMS isn't really his thing. It's a job, and as far as jobs go it's okay, but he's not going to retire a medic. "Shit, I would've quit like a year ago, but these girls, man? Damn. These girls." For now he's good where he is.

There are others. A couple of recent grads cycle through, people who had too much fun in college and need to bolster their résumés so they can get into med school. There are small-business owners—a contractor, a landscaper, a tax attorney—who need benefits and a steady paycheck during the lean months. There is a former cook and sommelier who has absolutely no idea how he ended up on an ambulance and wants out.

Among the Tourists, I finally begin to feel at home—that I can fit in, that I can last. They aren't freaks, they aren't scary, they don't know everything, they're doing a job. *Why* they chose this work over something else is because it's interesting. Each person has other things going on, and this job gives them just enough without getting in the way. From them, I learn that I can *be* here without being *of* here. I can be a dilettante. A Tourist.

"What the hell is that?"

My partner, a part-timer who's in and out so quickly that I never learn his name, says, "A balloon pump."

"And that's what, exactly?"

I'm standing in a stranger's living room. There's yellow shag carpet trampled to brown pulp by years of foot traffic; flowery wallpaper; and a TV but no couch. In fact, no furniture at all except a hospital bed, which has been wheeled in and made permanent—a double-wide trailer in miniature. Our patient is flopped on the bed. He has the soft, flabby look of a man who hasn't stood in a year, maybe more. He's in a diaper and smells like he gets nothing but sponge baths. He's attached to an IV pump and a feeding tube. He's been intubated, and machines breathe for him. Among other things, he's kept alive by something called a balloon pump.

My partner asks for the history, and the patient's around-the-clock nurse reads from a packet of papers. She mentions the balloon pump and the IV pump, rattles off medications and drip rates, diagnoses, complications, procedures. I don't understand any of it. I realize that for the last few months, I've gotten only a tiny peek at, taken the smallest bite of, this field. Until now, I've dealt with people having an acute and specific problem, people who—aside from having lost a few toes—are more or less healthy.

This is different.

Whatever confidence I've built up is gone. I back up and get out of the way, unsure what I'm supposed to do. I'm given very simple, direct instructions and still I screw it up.

The hospital, when we get there, is a relief. Get him out, walk away. Forget patients like this exist. It was tricky getting him onto our bed, and it'll be tricky getting him off. Nurses crowd the room; my partner confers with a doctor. An ER tech walks in. He sees that I'm overwhelmed and comes to take over the job I'm failing to do. "Mind if I get in here?"

I jump back, hands up. "Not at all, you're the pro."

"So what's that make you?"

He says it without looking, without breaking stride. *What's that make you?* It's not a question but an accusation. I want to explain that I'm here to have fun, to watch. A Tourist. But I realize in that instant how vacant the words are. The man on the bed is real, and so are all the devices keeping him alive. All of this is real. Except me. I've been sleepwalking through someone else's life.

This isn't new. Since graduating from college, I've been merely working a job. I've been present but never invested. There's been no passion, no professionalism, no dedication. I arrive on time and do what's required but nothing more. That attitude has carried through to EMS. Though I spent eight months in school, and though I nominally understand the responsibilities I've taken on, I've been going about my tasks without full commitment. I play along without joining up, I treat without caring. In not aiming to be better than good enough, I've been merely gawking. I'm a Peeping Tom.

11

The True Believer

Ultimately, it's Chris who leads me out of exile. Chris is a career medic, equal parts junkie and devotee. He's an EMS proselytizer, a True Believer. There will be no Tourists on his bus.

He's a member of the small but powerful contingent of medics who came of age in the back of an ambulance, which is an odd place to learn about the world. Chris, like all True Believers, is something of a savant. He can quickly and with great certainty determine whether a patient's shortness of breath is caused by asthma or congestive heart failure. He can also control a crowd, deliver a child, and stop even the heaviest of bleeding—but he can't find Norway on a map.

"No matter," he says. "I'm not here to save Norwegians."

He grew up wanting to be a medic. His first job after high school was with a tiny fire department in a rural county south of Atlanta. Chris drove the county's lone fire engine. It was so rural and the service was so small that it relied almost entirely on volunteers. When Chris was working, he'd be the only paid member on duty, meaning that once he relieved the guy who'd worked the day before, he'd be by himself in the fire station. He would eat, clean, watch TV, and sleep alone. He would also show up to calls alone, never knowing how many volunteers, if

any, would arrive to help. He stayed there for a while, then went
to paramedic school.

When he started working in the city in the mid-1990s, Atlanta was still a very rough place. The Olympics hadn't arrived
yet, and the first wave of scorched earth–style urban development and gentrification policies hadn't occurred yet. All of the
city's housing projects were still open, so at six P.M. the business-
men fled the city, leaving it to the homeless, the hookers, the
drugged out, the violent, and those too poor to escape. Drug
dealers were so in control, so brazen, that they'd set up shop anywhere they chose. On more than one occasion, medics would
emerge from an apartment only to find a drug deal going down
on the hood of their ambulance. The medics would watch idly as
the dealer exchanged brittle crack rocks for damp and crinkled
dollar bills, then wait until the junkie shuffled off and the dealer
swaggered back into the shadows before loading their patient.
One night a dozen Atlanta police officers crowded into an ambulance, drove it to a project, and carried out a surprise raid.
This temporarily broke the truce between EMS and the community, and for the better part of a year Chris wore a bulletproof
vest to work.

Whatever the dangers, the job was everything he'd hoped for.
One afternoon he found himself lying on the highway, slipping
a breathing tube down the trachea of a badly injured patient. He
paused to take stock of his situation—the wail of sirens, the dizzying smell of spilled gasoline mixed with the acrid smoke of a
car fire, the thrum of traffic in the southbound lane, the grooves
in the pavement below him—and couldn't believe this was his
luck, his job, his life.

After a few years on the street, he took a job at a children's hospital but returned to EMS when he was offered a supervisor's position. He was the one who noticed Jerry's girlfriend illegally running calls. Suddenly a medic slot was open on the busiest ambulance in South Fulton County. This moment came at a strange time in Chris's life. He'd been a medic for twelve years, had worked at fire departments, on ambulances, in hospitals, and as a supervisor. His marriage was on shaky ground. He'd reached the limits of what EMS could teach him. He was at the exact moment when the burned out either leave or turn into Killers. But Chris was a True Believer. For him there was nothing like being on an ambulance, having dinner interrupted by a shooting, being woken late at night to work a cardiac arrest, to laugh with the old and the infirm and the insane.

In all likelihood, he would have given up his supervisor's white shirt and jumped back on an ambulance eventually, but I hastened his decision. When he showed up that day and sniffed out Jerry's lie, he saw a young EMT, someone whose eyes were still wide to the wonder of EMS. Chris recognized an opportunity to start fresh, to love it again.

From day one, almost before Chris and I run our first call, EMS begins to click for me. Not merely as a distraction but as a career. As a calling. We laugh, we pull pranks, we run a shitload of calls. He leads patient care and I watch. He teaches me how to walk the fine line between exerting my authority and pissing people off, to casually check a patient's fingers for the telltale burn marks of a crack user, to begin clocking my path of escape—either with or without the patient—from the moment I arrive on-scene. Chris never says it, but the implication is clear: He's converting me into a True Believer.

12

Death by Broccoli

The dispatcher never stops talking. Talking to us, talking to other crews, talking to supervisors, occasionally talking to herself. Her voice is the one constant of this job, and though we hear everything she says, no words get our attention quite like *cardiac arrest*. Of all the calls we run, this one looms largest. A patient in cardiac arrest is essentially dead—his heart has stopped beating—but if we get there fast enough, we can change that. Working an arrest is our opportunity to not merely save a life but raise the dead.

By Thanksgiving, I still haven't run one. I'm brand-new and desperate to put my skills to use, and when you boil down that statement, what it really means is I'm hoping for something bad to happen to a perfect stranger. Morbid? Maybe. But it's going to happen anyway. I might as well be there when it does. So I wait. And I hope. I get frustrated.

Chris knows better. The holidays are approaching. People always die during the holidays. He says that in his ten-plus years of EMS, he can't recall a single major holiday when he hasn't worked a cardiac arrest. "Don't worry," he says. "We're due."

Thanksgiving starts out unusually quiet. The radio hardly makes a sound. We watch the parade, we watch football, we cook dinner. Just a few miles away, there is a family doing the same thing. They're a big group, brothers, sisters, aunts, uncles, cousins, Mom, Dad, even Dad's girlfriend. Grandma totters around the kitchen in a brightly colored muumuu, cooking and trying not to think about Granddad, who, stroked out and wearing diapers, is groaning on a mattress in the back bedroom. Two of her children have never gotten along. In years past, Granddad—tipsy but imperious—kept everyone in check. This year, emboldened by Granddad's absence, the brothers have argued nonstop.

They snap at each other over turkey, over stuffing, over sweet potatoes and collards and cheap wine. Grandma, now occupying the head of the table, stabs her fork into the broccoli and tells them to stop. This is Thanksgiving. Be happy, be nice. Be thankful. They get quiet just long enough for Grandma to stuff the entire floret of broccoli in her mouth. And then another dig. The younger brother, furious, yells back. Both men stand and Grandma slams her fork down. Mouth full of broccoli, she takes an ill-advised breath before telling them to stop, once and for all. This is the moment the family's been waiting for—Grandma, aging but in charge, throwing her significant weight around and putting these half-drunk men in their place.

But not a word comes. There's silence from the head of the table. A tangible silence that seems for the briefest of moments like the calm before the storm. Of course, there's no storm, just a desperate grunt, the final whiff of air sneaking out of Grandma's fully blocked airway. She bangs her hand on the table as the stringy, pulpy greenness that is death by broccoli becomes a very real possibility in her mind. The shouting stops, but only for an instant. There's confusion, recognition, shock, terror.

Then more shouting. Dishes and chairs are knocked over in the panic. Grandma's eyes go wide, mouth open. Her hands go to her throat, then, like a drowning swimmer, she flails, grabbing at anyone within reach.

Someone slaps her back. Fingers reach into Grandma's mouth—a desperate attempt to yank out the broccoli, which only loosens the dentures, which become yet another obstacle. Grandma's head bobs forward; her wig slips down over her face. She dies—loudly and ceremoniously—under the table during Thanksgiving dinner.

Someone dials 911.

No one tells us about the broccoli. All we hear is that someone's dead under the table and could we please hurry. And so we do, accompanied by a four-man fire crew aboard their engine. An ambulance rushing through the streets is not particularly dramatic; the truck itself is not imposing or intimidating, and the sirens, while loud, are not earsplitting. But a fire truck at full throttle is something altogether different. It's loud and terrible, ten thousand pounds of speeding menace with the lunatic wail of a screaming banshee. It's red-painted steel and a thousand gallons of sloshing water, a street-bound locomotive that can't stop, so get the hell out of its way, because it's coming. It's dangerous to the point of recklessness—a loaded gun in the hands of a felon—and seeing one in your rearview will make you move.

And so we drive. Sirens and blown intersections and me pushing pushing pushing to stay ahead of the engine, a gorilla breathing down our neck. Chris works the map book. In the days before GPS, this was as important and elusive a skill as any on the ambulance. A lot of people couldn't do it and got flustered and fucked it up. But Chris can work a map.

And so we arrive.

On the way there's conversation—about anything, about nothing—but once we're on-scene, it's deadly serious until we know what we have. A quick survey is all-important, and even when it's worse than expected, at least we know. There's solace in knowing. As soon as we pile out, I get hot. On the way here, driving, I'd gotten cold, almost to the point of a visible shiver. This is my tell, an invisible tic that surfaces every time I run a serious call. I get cold and remain cold until I arrive on-scene and then instantly warm up.

We hop out. Before I pull out the stretcher, Chris tells me to get a backboard. You can't do CPR on a mattress. The patient just sinks down with each compression. We need something firm to work against. I slide a backboard out from its chute, drop it on the stretcher, and Chris throws on the cardiac monitor, the drug bag, and an oxygen bottle. I yank the jump bag off the bench seat, and it goes on, too.

By now the firefighters have gathered next to us, and they help pull the stretcher out and push it up the driveway and toward the door. All the while, the family's yelling for us to hurry, screaming that she's dead and getting deader, but we can't run. Running is rushing and rushing is careless and the last thing anyone wants in this situation is carelessness.

Then it's through the front door and into the worst moment in a family's life. Death is seldom peaceful. It's loud and frantic, with lots of gurgling and thrashing and bodily fluids, all laid bare by the blinding light of panic. Standing helplessly and watching someone die is a terrifying experience, but when that person is your mother, the whole world spins at a different speed. We move through the house and pass a family in varying stages of grief—some crying, some screaming, some muttering, arms crossed tightly over their chest, walking in nervous little circles. Somewhere a toilet flushes.

Grandma is still under the table. Chris and a firefighter grab her ankles and yank her out. Suddenly guilty, suddenly caring, one of the two warring parties who started this whole thing yells for us to be careful, that she's his mother and how about we show some respect. This belated concern is the last bit of indignity his sister can handle. She flips out and begins slapping and clawing at him and has to be lifted up and carried outside. Chris grinds his knuckles into Grandma's chest, looking for a reaction, a sign of life, but her open and milky eyes never flicker.

Now for the muumuu. Her clothes have to be removed for us to slap on the paddles, but there's no way to get through such a large and billowing piece of fabric. It's all wound up and tangled like a wet parachute, and we struggle with it for a few seconds before someone cuts a four-inch slit down the center. Chris grabs one side, I grab the other, and we yank. It splits open to below her belly button, just low enough for us to learn that Grandma doesn't wear underwear. Chris flicks on the monitor, grabs the paddles, and places them on her chest—left hand over the breastplate, right along the ribs just below her heart. We all turn to the monitor and see the flowing V-shaped waves of a heart fluttering but not beating. Chris charges up the monitor.

This has a distinct sound, a high-pitched *bing* that mellows into a whine and culminates in a series of beeps—dee-doo-dee-doo-dee-doo, doot-doot—signifying the charge is ready. Chris yells clear. We all hold our hands up, and POP! Her body hops off the floor, back arching, head flopping. The monitor shows a brief run of the long, flat line that indicates the heart is no longer even quivering. Then, slowly, the V-shaped waves return. Chris increases the energy setting, recharges the monitor, yells clear, and POP. Another jerk. Another flat stretch of nothingness, then the waves return. Again he ups the energy setting. Again he charges the paddles. Again he yells clear and shocks her. Still no change.

A firefighter drops to his knees and begins CPR—a traumatic, almost obscene assault on the body. Two hands over the breastplate, arms locked, an unending string of compressions delivered with the full force of a grown man. The breastplate quickly breaks free from the ribs; the connecting cartilage snaps with each compression and makes a percussive pop like thick ice breaking deep below the surface. Chris reaches into the jump bag and pulls out the airway kit. I shuffle along on my knees and take hold of Grandma's hand. It's time for an IV.

There's never been any proof that drugs actually help patients in cardiac arrest, but still we give them. Call it better dying through pharmaceuticals. There's epinephrine, which hits the heart like a brushfire, a frantic and hysterical scream for it to do something, anything. Behind it, playing the role of good cop, is amiodarone. It eases in gentle as bathwater, a calming voice to whisper that everything will be all right. They simultaneously alert and reassure the heart: *Just follow us and everything will be okay.*

I straighten out Grandma's arm but can't find a vein. The thing about someone in arrest is, basically, she's dead. There's no blood flowing, so the veins are flat and hard to find. I wrap a tourniquet around her upper arm, swab the area with alcohol, and, seeing nothing, plunge the needle in. Tissue that isn't getting blood has the consistency of Play-Doh. The patient is, after all, just an official time of death away from being a cadaver. I keep digging, but before I can find anything, Chris waves me over.

He has the airway kit open and half the tools out—syringes and tubes and tape and blades—in a big jumbled mess around him. He wipes his forehead with the back of his hand and says something isn't right. He's having trouble seeing down into Grandma's airway. Something's in there. I ask if he wants to try the suction, and he nods. "Yeah, let's give it a shot."

This is one of those moments when the reality of trying to save lives on an ambulance hits home. We don't have fancy battery-powered suction units like the hospitals do. What we have is a piece of hollow plastic—long skinny tip on one end, accordion in the middle, trigger on the handle. If Chris squeezes fast enough and long enough, it may create enough suction. We're skeptical. Chris starts squeezing the trigger, working the accordion in and out—fffi-fffoo fffi-fffoo. He's not getting anything out, but he keeps going—fffiffi-fffoo fffi-fffoo fffi-fffoo. Now the family's watching and whispering—*What the hell is that noise?* Fffiffi-fffoo fffi-fffoo fffi-fffoo.

Chris is in a full-on sweat when it works. He's shocked, I'm shocked. He pulls the suction out, and there, wedged into the hollow tip, is an entire floret of broccoli. The stem is stamped with a single set of teeth marks. "You gotta be shitting me," Chris whispers. We look from the broccoli to each other and back.

Obstacle clear, he slips the tube down her throat and secures it with tape. It's time to go. There are more shocks to deliver, more CPR to do, meds to give. But really, it's over. Everything we've done in the last twenty minutes has had absolutely no effect, which generally isn't a very good sign. We snatch the patient and all of our equipment and hustle outside. Two firefighters hop in the back with Chris, extra hands to do compressions and give ventilations as he shocks and pushes drugs.

As we're about to leave, a niece asks if she can come. This is a tough call. An ambulance is a small place, and if she starts flipping out, there's nothing I can do about it short of kicking her out on the highway. But she seems calm, so I open the door for her. She climbs in, buckles her seat belt, and then lets out a tortured wail that continues, at varying volume, until we arrive at the hospital.

Inside we're greeted by a coterie of doctors and nurses. Chris gives a report and the staff checks our interventions. Nothing we've done has helped, and they quickly wind down their efforts. Just as quickly as it began, it's over. Her time of death is 19:23.

Broccoli has claimed another victim.

I head outside to clean and restock the ambulance. I'm sweeping up, lost in thought, when I step on Grandma's dentures. The floor of an ambulance is steel, and the teeth break under my weight with a loud ceramic crack. I walk inside, the broken dentures in two pieces in my hand, and find the niece. She's quiet now, much calmer than she was in the ambulance. I hold my hand out, do my best to look her in the eye, and explain that I broke the teeth. She nods, takes them into her own hands, and thanks me for everything I've done to help. I'm not sure I deserve forgiveness, let alone praise, but I tell her she's more than welcome. I want to cry. I want to hug her. I want to be on an ambulance for the rest of my life.

13

The Seekers

"**D**oes it matter if the patient lives?"

Chris, behind the wheel, takes his eyes off the road. "Damn," he says. "Damn."

I feel the subtle tug of the ambulance losing momentum as he takes his foot off the gas. His arms go limp as he lets go of the wheel. We're now coasting down the road, neither of us looking to see where we're going. "Damn," he says again. I nod, very proud of my question. He thinks about it, comes to no conclusion, and resumes driving.

It's early spring, about five o'clock. Outside, the evening sky is deep purple and soft orange, the way it always is in April in the South. Trees are blooming. Bugs, birds—they're all coming back out. The humidity that will soak everything in a suffocating closeness hasn't arrived. It is, for the moment, perfect. And that's what we're discussing—perfection in the form of a 911 call. It's a frequent topic of conversation for us, something we discuss over breakfast, over dinner, late at night. Sometimes, when we're both asleep, one of us will pop up and throw out a suggestion. What happens if he bleeds on you, pukes on you, if you slip in his growing puddle of piss? And if it really were the Perfect Call, then would you eat there?

We discuss when in the shift it would have to happen and settle on midnight. Then there's the question of what resources we'd need at our disposal, how many patients would be involved, and what type of call—medical or trauma—it would be. We agree that we'd be on our own, no help close enough to be called in, nothing to rely on but ourselves. And it would have to be a trauma call. On Christmas we ran our second cardiac arrest together. It was frantic—a *shit-kicker*, is what people call it—because the woman was only having an asthma attack when we arrived. I was the first one through the door and found her sitting on the couch—sweat-drenched, hands on her knees, eyes bugging out, mouth wide in an attempt to suck in air. She looked at me, desperate, and gasped, "Don't let me die!"

Then she died.

We dragged her to the entryway and started CPR, and shortly after that, the fire department came and helped us get her to the ambulance. We shocked her heart back into activity, but she never regained consciousness, and after a minute or two her heart went south again and never recovered. Because it was all happening in front of us—first talking, then not talking, then not breathing, then heart not beating, then heart beating, then not beating again—it was messy and complicated, and we had to keep changing tactics and drugs and procedures, and it came so, so close.

Somewhere during the shifts between dead and not dead, it struck me that this had almost all the earmarks of the Perfect Call. I looked up to say it only to find Chris looking at me with a lunatic smile and realized he'd had the same thought. This was *so close*. But not quite. It was just her, and there was no carnage.

So it couldn't be a purely medical call. There'd have to be

blood and bones and maybe even charred remains. It couldn't be purely trauma, either. A pure trauma call means there's nothing for us to do but stop the bleeding and hurry to the hospital. It leaves all the fun to the surgeons, and fuck them, anyway. No, it would have to be all-encompassing. There'd have to be a few dead people on the scene for us to gawk at and patients who would rapidly die of their injuries without immediate intervention, *our* intervention. *Multiple mechanism* is a phrase we invent and stick to—maybe a car wreck that starts a fire and pushes someone off a bridge. Or a gunshot that passes through the first guy's head (killing him) and then nicks the next guy's liver before hitting a gas tank and igniting the entire scene in a giant orange blaze, a funeral pyre from which we rescue the wounded. Or don't.

And that's the question. Does the patient have to live for it to be the Perfect Call? Further complicating the issue is whether a good call can be elevated to Perfect Call status if we save the patient. Does saving a life trump all the other elements?

In the end, we decide the answer is no. The patient doesn't have to live for it to be the Perfect Call. And no, getting a save doesn't elevate a good call to a Perfect Call. We reason that we didn't cause the problem—we weren't the ones who sped without a seat belt or overdosed on heroin or came out on the losing end of a murder-suicide, and we sure as hell weren't the ones who dialed 911 and opened the door. We're the ones who show up. And really, the Perfect Call isn't about the patient. It's about us. It's about the experience, and for the patient, the experience is going to suck regardless. So a mundane call in which the patient lives because of our efforts doesn't trump a real shit-kicker even if the patient dies. As long as we get there first, outperform the expectations, and do it fast and in the most extreme conditions, nothing else matters. Not every patient is going to live, so why should a death bring down the party?

And for us, it is a party. Chris and I have been partners for eight months; we're not just coworkers now but friends. We hang out after work, I attend his daughter's birthday party, meet his family. For twenty-four hours every third day, each of us is all the other has. We have the same sense of humor and complement each other in a Laurel and Hardy kind of way. I'm tall and lean; he's a man of considerable size. He's constantly in search of a bathroom. I can't poop in public. He's incredibly charming. My dry, sarcastic humor leaves people offended. He's rarely left the Southeast; I've been to Asia three times. He's an incredibly competent medic; I'm an eager pupil.

Having decided on the Perfect Call, we actively set out to find it. Management has divided South Fulton County into five zones, each manned by a different ambulance and each with its own flavor. The supervisor's office is in Zone One. For everyone else, showing up at work means being totally on one's own, but the Zone One crews sleep one sheet of drywall away from their boss. Because they can't get away with anything, the crews here either exist as rule followers or get banished. The general rule is "Don't fuck around in Zone One."

Zone Four is known for being quiet—two-calls-a-shift quiet—and attracts the lazy and the burned out. The coolest zone by far is Five. It includes Fulton Industrial Boulevard, which is nothing but factories, truck stops, strip clubs, and cheap motels. The factories and warehouses provide plenty of trauma, and the truck drivers provide everything else imaginable. If Fulton Industrial is any indication, long-haul trucking must be a lonely and strange existence. The truckers attract drugs and hookers—cheap, mean, toothless hookers carrying box cutters and strange tropical diseases. The hookers attract more drugs, mostly meth, and that attracts dealers and users and stickup men and drifters.

Zone Three is forgettable.

Chris and I are in Zone Two, which is the busiest in the entire county, north or south. We serve a large residential population, but Zone Two is defined by two streets: Godby Road and Old National Highway.

Godby is short and filthy and crowded end to end with old housing projects slowly sinking into the clay. Old National is a busy four-lane crowded with shady check-cashing huts and fast-food chains. The Red Lobster is always packed. At night Club Twenty Grand and its neighbor, the Ice Palace, take over, and the street fills with pimped-out cars and motorcycles smoking their tires.

From the perspective of my Rural/Metro colleagues, Zone Two is the worst posting in Fulton, but Chris and I love it. We never sleep, never go to the station. We prowl the streets at cruising speed, not only waiting for calls but daring them to happen. We troll the projects late at night or idle outside one of the clubs. We buy a disposable camera and, at every opportunity, hop out and take our picture with whatever oddity we come across. The guy in the Uncle Sam costume dancing outside of a tax office, a singing junkie who's just gotten a fix, the hookers who wander over to ask for Band-Aids or gauze or a couple of spare bedsheets.

Every crew carries a clipboard, and in it, aside from paperwork, is the patient pen. We never touch the patient pen except to clean it. Patients never touch our pen. When a document needs to be signed, we open the clipboard and offer them the patient pen. We found ours at a gas station. It was in a rack up front, in a clear plastic box filled with gag gifts. It's supposed to be a big fat finger—long and fat and fleshy pink—but it looks more like a penis, and every time we hand it to people, they pick it up tentatively, holding it as if it might explode. Which it does. It's a farting pen, a play on the old pull-my-finger joke. When you grip it, the pen lets out a long electronic fart. Watching a person's face when he grabs this dildo-shaped writing utensil and hears its flatulence is too much. Especially at two in the morning.

Because we're always moving, we're within striking distance of everything, and if a decent call drops anywhere near us, we jump on it whether it's in our zone or not. One afternoon we're miles into Zone Three—Chris has to crap and is starting to sweat, but he's partial to the bathroom in Target—when a call goes out for a man who's collapsed on a roof. It sounds exciting. Chris forgets about the toilet and grabs the radio to tell the crew we'll handle it. Scaling buildings and shuffling along rooftops is more of a fire department thing, but we arrive first. So we pare our equipment down to the absolute necessities and climb up. Turns out the guy is a diabetic passed out from low blood sugar. Crouching on the hot shingles, I start an IV as Chris runs the medicine through a bag of saline fluid. It's the highlight of our day—a sick patient, a nervous crowd of onlookers two stories below, the inherent danger of practicing medicine on a roof— and we decide we'll never again let a good call go without at least making an attempt to get there.

Most crews don't mind being told they can go back to sleep or keep eating or doing whatever it was they were doing, but occasionally someone complains or a supervisor asks how we could possibly be so close to a call so deep into someone else's zone. These are questions that could lead to trouble, but Chris is a made guy, a rising star in the organization, and we take advantage of his status as former supervisor and friend of the director. We slip in and out of our zone with impunity, always driving, two sharks patrolling the ocean, ignoring every rule that could slow us down.

14

Two Dead at Midnight

"I just put my hand in brain."

"What'd it feel like?"

"Squishy."

Old National—the four-lane road in our territory—is congested and dangerous because no one pays attention to the pedestrians. It consumes everything on two feet, rich and poor, like a bear gone mad with hunger. It has an open median down the middle, and one night the median claims two for itself.

The setup is simple, one of those things you'd never think about until it happens, and once it does, you wonder why it doesn't happen more often, why it's never happened to you. Two people cross the road. It's late, midnight, and very dark. They don't use the crosswalk. They simply wait for a break in traffic and start going. Halfway across, in the median, they stop and wait for another opening. It never comes. A car preparing for a left turn swings into the median and slams into them both. The driver reacts, but it's too late. They're hit, they're broken, they're tossed in the air. They—and the various bits of them—land here and there.

Chris and I are the first to arrive. A loud, fast, screaming response. The rule for scenes with multiple patients is first in, last out. As first in, the carnage is ours to survey. It's up to us to call in the appropriate resources, to determine whose injuries require treatment and who can be left to die. Triage is a brutal process of deciding who can't be saved so resources can be focused elsewhere. Any patient found without a pulse will remain pulseless; we'll leave him and move on. Sometimes that person we found twitching, eyes wide and not breathing, the one we left for dead, sometimes he starts breathing again. Startled but not surprised, we upgrade him from dead to critical and he gets transported. No hard feelings, my friend. Sometimes life finds a way.

There's no such confusion tonight. The first patient we come across, horribly injured and, in all likelihood, doomed, is alive. Chest like a bag of gravel—ribs, sternum, collarbones, all broken. Her lungs are punctured, and huge pockets of air are filling the void. We jab two long, wide needles in, a vain attempt to let some of the trapped air out, but it's just an afterthought. The legs are also broken, probably from the bumper. They do that, bumpers—snap the bones so they flop and fold like a doll's legs.

Help arrives and the first patient is spirited away—alive, but how long that will last, well . . .

The other patient isn't. Isn't alive, isn't a patient, isn't someone to be treated. He was launched over the hood, struck his head on the driver's-side corner of the windshield, and was thrown back down. He's lying in the glare of the headlights, skull open, face obscured by scalp. There's nothing to do but look. Which we can do. Because of the headlights. From the car. Which has a driver.

Shit.

I walk over to the passenger side and signal for the driver to roll his window down. He's behind the wheel, unblinking eyes staring out through the punched-in windshield. He's frozen, he's silent. He's covered in hair. This man—whose only crime was to be behind the wheel when someone else made a poor choice—has killed two people and now sits covered in their hair. How long will he feel the prickly stab of shorn hair on his exposed skin? It's a horrible situation for everyone involved, and this guy is in need of some sort of attention.

"Are you okay?"

He looks at the form slumped in the glare of his headlights, at his punched-in windshield, at the hair. He doesn't answer. He doesn't have to. I want to tell him it isn't his fault, that it could've happened to anyone, that he's the unlucky winner of the worst lottery ever. I put my hand on the roof, start to lean in the window, and realize I'm touching not cold steel but, rather, a warm, wobbly bowl of Jell-O—except it isn't. It's a brain, and I've put my hand right in it.

I stand up. Peel off my glove. Thank God for gloves. Then I walk over to Chris, a little pale, a little repulsed, a little amused. He crinkles his forehead as if to say, *What?*

"I just put my hand in brain."

15

Nailed to the Wall

In a job where it's possible to scoop up a stranger's brain, it's important to have levity. But after a while, I lose the ability to judge which stories to tell my friends and which go beyond the limits of good taste. Death cracks inside jokes that only we emergency workers—with our practical knowledge of the post-mortem human—will ever laugh at.

I learn, for instance, to leave the room immediately when a rookie cop starts to roll a bloated body, because it's guaranteed to burst. And without having to be told, I know that when you fish a floater out of a pond, you should never hook an extremity—it'll always rip off. Chris and I laugh at these things because we've watched them happen, and what we've seen once, we're bound to see again. It is Santayana's maxim turned on its head, then dunked in formaldehyde and filtered through crime scene tape: Those who know the lessons of decomposition are condemned to witness them repeatedly.

There will always be another dead body, another fetid roach-infested house. We will never escape the smells, the fluids, the unwashable *ick* of people deep in the throes of a communicable disease. We've run these calls—the disgusting, the foul—and we'll run them again. So when Darryl comes along, nobody complains. Not that it's dinnertime, not that it's been a busy day and we're exhausted, not that it's a Saturday during college football season and all the good games are about to start. We take him as a gift, payback for the roach-filled houses and the late-night calls and the three sweltering hours we recently devoted to hosing the ambulance clean of blood and bits left over from the guy who'd blown his brains out in his parents' basement. Like Martin Sheen in *Apocalypse Now,* we asked for a great call, and for our sins we're given Darryl, a drunk redneck living in a black neighborhood who on this day has nailed himself to the wall.

Darryl lives with Tammy, his common-law wife, in a duplex with yellowing plaster walls. The place is beat up and looks like it should be left to the possums. I grab the spotlight, point it at the tin numbers tacked to the door, and double-check them against the ones we've been given by dispatch. I always double-check the numbers. There's a guy—well, there *was* a guy—who got called out to a person down. When no one answered after the second knock, he kicked in the front door only to find himself face-to-face with the patient's very pissed-off neighbors.

Even out in the street with the ambulance windows open, we can hear the yelling. There are different kinds of yells, each advertising a peculiar set of circumstances. The shrill yelling of genuine pain; the cracked-voice yelling of someone who's been wronged; and the ghost moan of those left brokenhearted. And then there's the angry, violent yelling of a domestic dispute. There's nothing more dangerous and unpredictable than a domestic. A wife beaten half to death becomes a knife-wielding lunatic the second her husband is placed in custody.

Still, we go in. Tammy—all sunburn and skinny legs and rolling, unapologetic belly—meets us at the door. She hooks a grimy thumb toward the house. "Jackass nailed hisself to the wall," she says.

Chris nods. "Well, let's have a look."

We pick our way around piles of faded jeans, muddy sneakers, tool belts, and porn magazines—the grand total of Darryl's existence—until we reach the bedroom. And there, as promised, is Darryl. Nailed to the wall. He instantly focuses his attention on us. "Please, sir, please. You gotta help me, sir. Please."

Darryl stands just inside the bedroom door, a single nail through his left elbow attaching him to the wall. There's a nail gun at his feet. Tammy pokes her head in. "I already told you, Darryl. I don't love you no more."

Chris taps the wall. The nail has gone through a stud. Darryl isn't concerned about the wall. "Sir, can I talk to you? For a second, sir?"

"Did you really mean to do this?"

Darryl nods. "Okay, sir. Okay. I ain't even gonna lie to you, sir. I ain't even gonna lie. I been drinking. Had me two beers."

Two beers, incidentally, is the magic number. Every staggering homeless man, every puke-covered lawyer, every passed-out college girl, they all have one thing in common: They've had exactly two drinks today.

Darryl burps, swallows hard. "It's a weakness, but I'm working on it. I been askin' the Lord to help me out with it."

Tammy's back. "You better ask the Lord to help you get your stupid ass unnailed from that wall! Otherwise you'll be stuck here watchin' me and Todd consummate my new life!"

And there it is. Tammy has met someone new and wants Darryl gone. Drunk and unable to let go of the skinny-legged, sunburned love of his misguided life, Darryl nailed himself to the wall. Given the choice between a nail through the elbow and being an unwilling spectator at the Tammy and Todd Show, I'm not sure which I'd choose. If not for us, Darryl, the poor bastard, would've gotten both.

As engrossing as all this is, there's only one option: Fire up a saw and cut him out. Darryl overhears us talking and starts shaking his head, his voice trembling. "No, sir. No way in hell. You can't cut this wall. This wall cannot be cut. This wall is like the bond of love, and there ain't nothin' can cut through the bond of love!"

Twenty minutes later, the fire department has cut through the wall. Now we have other problems. Darryl, drunk as hell and suddenly free, is stomping around with a three-foot-by-three-foot section of Sheetrock nailed to his arm. The cops tell him to relax, to sit down and shut up and go to the hospital. "Get that thing off your arm," they say. "Sober up and sort this out tomorrow." It's sensible, but Darryl is in no mood for sensible. The cops are invited, cordially, to suck his dick.

And here come the cuffs.

I could have predicted what happens next: Darryl refuses to go peacefully, and Tammy—the woman who threatened to sleep with another man while her nailed-to-the-wall common-law husband watched—experiences a change of heart. She is now Darryl's defender. She punches a cop.

When it's all over and the screaming has stopped, when the clouds of pepper spray have drifted off into the night, the final score looks something like this: Tammy is melting down in the back of a patrol car; two cops, having wandered into the cloud of pepper spray, are crying and staggering around; the neighbors—all black, all amused—have turned out to see what the crazy crackers are up to; and Darryl? He's in the back of our ambulance, the three-foot-by-three-foot section of wall still nailed to his arm. He's sitting quietly on the stretcher.

After the door closes, he smiles, crosses his legs like he's in a lounge chair instead of an ambulance, and shakes his head. He asks me, "You got you a woman?"

I nod.

"Treat her right, man. Treat her right. Ain't nothin' in the world like a good woman. Not a damn thing. And I oughta know. Got me the best one there is."

16

Accidental Veterinarians

That Darryl makes us laugh, even though it's *at* him and not *with* him, means he's one of the good guys. For all the nonsense, the yelling, the rolling cloud of pepper spray, it was fun, and as far as I'm concerned, Darryl's all right. Call any time, brother. But for every Darryl, there are a thousand others who yell, curse, spit, or—just as bad—sit on the floor and demand to be carried down the stairs because they have a cold and we're here to serve.

Chris is always saying he prefers dogs to humans. Dogs are loyal, humans are a pain in the ass. I tend to agree. Still, it never occurred to me that I'd be dispatched to save a dog. Until today.

It's late June, not even ten in the morning, and already I'm sweating. This is nothing: Atlanta is a steam engine in the summer, nothing but humidity, and whatever today brings is a mere suggestion of what's to come in August. It's been a quiet morning, and no sooner do I say this—as if in punishment for even thinking the thought—than our radio chirps.

"Seven-oh-four, I have a call for you."

We're flying down the road, sirens wailing. The dispatcher is giving us constant updates, and her voice, normally calm and indifferent, is just this side of shrill. We've been dispatched to a two-year-old actively choking. Nobody likes running calls on kids. Not only are they young and innocent, they're small, and working on a child is like writing with your left hand— essentially the same act but awkward and much more difficult than it has to be.

We're a few minutes from the address when the radio crackles again and the dispatcher says we can cancel. The patient, the one who's choking, it's a dog. I flip off the siren. The lights. We slow down. Chris is looking at me, and I know what he's thinking: *I like dogs more than I like most people.* Why not?

We pull up to a run-down little house, unpainted, with a sagging roof. There's no grass; the front lawn is nothing but clay. Weeds fan out for acres from the other three sides. Standing on the porch in a housedress and slippers is the smallest, oldest woman I've ever seen. We hop out. She's nervous but not overly excited and tells us she tossed a T-bone to her dog, JJ, and he swallowed it. Whole.

Chris looks around. "How big is JJ?"

"Pretty big," she says.

There's a doghouse in the middle of the yard, and next to it is a four-foot stake driven two feet into the clay. A chain thick enough to tow a barge is wrapped around the stake and pulled tight. It stretches across the yard and disappears into the weeds.

"He on the end of that?" Chris asks.

"'Less he broke it again."

"He can break that?"

"If he has a mind to."

"He mean?"

"Depends."

And just like that, the chain goes slack. JJ is coming home. I start to sweat. Chris backs up. JJ bursts through the weeds like a rampaging elephant. A gray pit with the head of a tiger shark and the muscled shoulders of a Spanish bull. Every ounce of ninety pounds. We're well within his perimeter, and there's no time to react. He's on us before we even hear the rattle of his heavy chain. He jumps and—to both our relief and our shock—lands on his side, just short of us, with a heavy thud. He digs furiously at his mouth with his front paws, scrambles to his feet, eyes wild, then throws himself down again. He knows he's dying, and he's terrified.

Choking is a scary thing. Imagine being wide awake but unable to breathe, fully alert and fully aware that this is it. To find a comparably miserable death, you'd have to be eaten or beaten or burned alive. Choking is violent and desperate right up until the moment it isn't—that moment being death.

JJ's not there, but he's close. We have to do something, but we have no idea what. Were he a person and not a dog, this would be so much easier. I'd simply place a hand on his shoulder and ask, "Are you choking?" Seriously. That's the first step of the Heimlich, to approach the patient and make sure he is, in fact, choking. Imagine the look of abject terror on the choker's face temporarily being replaced by the shocked and put-out expression of pure frustration. If he can manage a grunt or a wheeze— even if he says, "I'm choking"—he's not choking. For those who are choking, whose airway is so blocked that they can't squeeze out so much as a syllable, we start the Heimlich. If the patient is human. Which JJ isn't. He's a dog. A big one.

And so how do you save a creature that might, once saved, tear you apart? I look at Chris. He looks at me. There's no manual for saving dogs, no canine Heimlich, no precedent of any kind for how to deal with a giant choking dog. But he's choking.

I drop the bag, fall to my knees, peek into his huge mouth. Beyond the muscular jaws, beyond the rows of teeth, beyond the enormous flapping tongue, I can see the bone. He swallowed it whole. Imagine a T-bone divested of meat. The thick crossbar running sideways up top, the long, skinny shaft curving down. The shaft is in his throat, and the crossbar is stuck at the back of his mouth. He's desperate and furious, and getting it out means reaching into the area most likely to do us serious damage.

Chris doesn't want to do it. Neither do I. JJ is massive. That mouth, those teeth. But he's panicking. And choking. We inch closer. At our approach, JJ—still on his side—thumps his tail against the clay. We're obligated to help. Maybe not as medics but as people. Chris grabs the forceps, asks how we're going to do this.

"I thought you had a plan."

"Do I look like I have a plan?"

"You have the forceps."

He holds them out. "You want 'em?"

"No."

JJ is back up, head shaking, desperate. He flops down and tries to get up again but can't. How much time we have, how blocked his airway is, we don't know. We also don't know how he'll react to us shoving our hands in his mouth. He spins frantically in the clay, and the old woman whimpers. Since we have no plan, we don't bother discussing it. I simply jump on JJ, straddle him, and try like hell to hold him still. It's like wrestling a freight train. Chris reaches in with the forceps. I hear the clink of metal on teeth, a garbled cough, the furious thump of tail against clay. The old woman is praying now—"Praise Jesus! Thank you, Lord Jesus!" JJ's eyes go wide and zero in on me. Chris can get up at any time and run. I'm in the compromised position of spooning a totally freaked-out ninety-pound pit bull whose mouth, at any moment, will be violently set free. I have no exit strategy.

Chris grunts, swears, jumps to his feet, and yells for me to get up. I don't think, I just move. I'm on my feet and backpedaling almost before I realize it. "Did you get it?"

"No."

"Is he still choking?"

"I don't think so."

JJ is up, legs wide, panting, head swinging from side to side. The T-bone is out of his airway but stuck in his mouth. An improvement but not a cure. And that's as good as it's gonna get. I ask the old woman if she has a vet. She nods. We dust our pants off while she starts the car, and once she's ready for us, we grab JJ. He dips his head toward his left shoulder like he's going to play. His tail wags. A truce. I ease over, grab his collar, and unclip the chain. Then we walk him to the car, lift him up, and put him in the back. With two quick hops, he's plopped down in the passenger seat.

"JJ! Get in the back!" the old woman yells.

But JJ isn't budging. He almost died, and now that he hasn't, he's going to soak it all in. It's the front seat or nothing from here on out.

17

(Un)Prepared for the Worst

Chris has just eaten Chik-fil-A, and it's starting to talk to him. Gas, cold sweats. Evidently the cramps have begun, because he's fidgeting now. He's gotta go. But he can't.

"How long do we have to stay?" he asks, practically levitating in the passenger seat.

"According to the memo? It's gonna be a while."

We're one of two Fulton County EMS crews assigned to participate in a disaster-preparedness exercise. Someone has set off a dirty bomb. We're surrounded by radiation, and the casualties—the dead, the dying, the slowly melting—are everywhere. It's all fake, part of some federally mandated program to see how well we've incorporated the lessons of 9/11. In short, should the worst (re)occur, how will the first responders respond?

Not well, evidently. Communications are nonexistent, and at least three different people have claimed to be in charge. Patients are scattered about, and no effort has been made to separate them by severity. Worse yet, every medic, cop, and firefighter taking part in the exercise has either willfully or accidentally wandered into the radiation cloud. We're all melting.

None of which concerns Chris. "I mean, seriously. Who

stages an event like this without giving any consideration to a bathroom?"

I shrug. "Surprise, surprise, the government shit the bed."

"Yeah, well, I'm about to shit my pants." He swings his door open. "I'm going to the dollar store. Anybody wants to see a real mass-casualty incident, tell 'em I'll be in the men's room. Third stall. Show these idiots what a dirty bomb really looks like."

After he leaves, things only get worse. The fire department's decontamination tent collapses. Half the patients get bored and wander off. A car chase lures away nearly all the cops providing crowd control. And then, finally, the mess becomes a full-fledged clusterfuck.

"Where's Chris?" Our supervisor is sweating and agitated, screaming like this isn't a drill but the real thing.

"Bathroom."

"Bathroom? What the hell's he doing in the bathroom?"

"Well, uh, I believe he said he had to—"

"Get him back here! Now!"

Turns out the first ambulance to leave the scene—stuffed with more than a dozen patients—has broken down. Now our supervisor can't find it, can't make radio contact, nothing. It simply disappeared. Chris is laughing when he emerges from the bathroom. He laughs as we load our own batch of radioactive patients. And he keeps laughing until we reach the hospital, where, abruptly, he stops. Nearly every nurse, doctor, and janitor on staff is in the parking lot. They are scared, angry, and confused. Evidently no one has told them this is just a drill, that the county is staging a disaster, and that they, the ER staff of the closest hospital, will receive the patients. For them today was just another day until words like *dirty bomb* and *radiation* and *mass casualties* began crackling over their med radio. Suddenly, ambulances were on the way with something horrible, something they weren't prepared for.

When it's all over, after we've been chewed out by the doctors, after the fire department has officially given up on their decon tent, after the radiation cloud has drifted off and killed the entire city, we're released. On our way back to the station, we pass the missing ambulance. It's strapped to the back of a tow truck like a sad, wounded animal. What became of the patients, I have no idea.

A week later, we receive our grade: room for improvement, but overall, not bad. Though we aren't prepared to save ourselves, let alone anyone else, we're good enough. That government at all levels is rubber-stamping disaster response and sentencing our preparedness to death by mediocrity isn't surprising. In fact, it's so much like *M*A*S*H,* I can't help but laugh. So long as it remains in the abstract. Though nothing ever does.

A few months later, Sabrina and I visit New York City and go to the 9/11 museum at Ground Zero. A sign at the door says soldiers, police, and firefighters are given free admittance. I ask the girl at the ticket counter if EMTs, too, get in free. She shrugs and says no. Free admission is only for people whose sacrifices on that day—and every day since—the museum is meant to honor. And she has a point.

I don't fight fires, and I'm not in the military. I've never been deployed. Never taken incoming rocket fire. I've never fired a shot in anger or been forced to watch my friends die. And though on occasion I've narrowly escaped death, it's not a daily threat. And so I'm not a warrior, wounded or otherwise. I don't have a medal, a prosthetic, PTSD.

What I do have is a scuff on the toe of my right boot. It's a reminder. Not of the kid who was shot dead. Not that it was done execution-style and we found him facedown on the grass. Not that it was a large-caliber handgun that punched in the back of his skull and erased his forehead. Not that when I rolled him over, his face flopped down like congealed cheese off lukewarm pizza. Not that his brain slithered out into the wet grass. It's a reminder of the curb, the one I nervously but gently kicked when his father came out. The one I dug my foot into as this man staggered over, vomited, and collapsed onto the driveway. The one I hid behind when he rose to his knees and wailed—bone-deep and pitch-perfect, humanity's enduring anguish. I got that scuff there, barely three miles from home and four hours from the end of my shift. I got it waiting for a father swallowed up by his own grief to calmly and, in a voice I could understand, tell me his son's full name. I got it because death, even horrific death, requires paperwork. I got it because it happened on my shift, and it was my job to get it.

Sabrina is as offended as I am. And why not? It's her husband who, well intentioned but unprepared, will wander into a radioactive cloud. That some of us who wore this uniform never made it home is personal for her. More than I realized. And in her mind, if their sacrifice doesn't merit free admission, they should at least be remembered.

Counted among those killed in the World Trade Center on September 11, 2001, were forty-three paramedics and EMTs.

Godspeed.

18

Death Before Discharge

The Fulton County Department of Public Health is a strange place to have an existential crisis, but here I am. Three days ago I was stuck with a dirty needle, and now I'm waiting on the results of my blood test. The possibility that I could be killed on the job has always been there, however remote, but that it could happen like this? By accident? A simple mistake on a routine call? It's an insult. All the more so because it will be willfully ignored, because if even the 9/11 EMS dead don't rate remembrance, what then of a lonely EMT who dies from a needle stick? So what I want to know—aside from whether I have hepatitis or AIDS—is whether it's worth it.

Is it?

That I'd question whether a job is worth dying for hints at the myriad of ways I've changed, at how strange a year this has been. Looking at it now, I can see the signs. They've been there a while, I just had no reason to step back and take stock. Now that I have, I'd say the first hint that things were different—that life wouldn't, couldn't, go back to the way it used to be—was the day I found a skull fragment in my boot.

We'd run a shooting near the end of the shift, a gruesome but fairly standard dead guy with the left side of his head blown off.

His skull was obliterated, and the skin hung slack like a dodge ball with the air let out. There was nothing to do but look. He'd bled everywhere, and I was careful not to step in anything, but evidently not careful enough. For the last hour of the shift, I heard a faint click with every other step, like something small but hard—a pebble, perhaps—was stuck in the tread of my right boot. I was tired, and it had been a long day, so I ignored it until I got home, where it wasn't a click I heard but a scratch. The pebble was damaging the wood floor. Sabrina heard it first, though by that time I'd been walking around for ten minutes. I sat in a chair, pulled off my boot, and pried out what looked like a small piece of broken glass. It was thick and off-white, a shard from a broken plate, maybe. Except it wasn't. It was a skull fragment I'd stepped on at the shooting scene. I'd carried it around and brought it home, and here it was. In my hand. I laughed and said we should keep it. Sabrina wasn't amused. I apologized and promised not to wear my boots in the house. Then I flung the fragment into the neighbor's yard.

The second sign that I'd evolved into someone else? My new take on the Volkswagen Beetle. Chris and I spend an incredible amount of time kneeling in the street. Ostensibly we're treating patients, but really what we're doing is listening for—and occasionally hearing—the scream of tires as a car flies around the corner. Chris and I agree that the terrifying prospect of death by automobile is amplified by the fact that we know exactly what the car would do to our bodies: how the bones will break, where we'll land, which of the sleepy medics from Zone Three will marvel at having accidentally touched our brains.

Maybe it's a defense mechanism, maybe it's a gradual desensitizing, but we've developed a game: Of all the cars on the road,

which one would you least like to be killed by? Chris says something big, a truck, maybe, with a plow on the front that would
splatter him into unrecognizable paste to be hosed into the gut-
ter by the fire department. For me it's the Beetle. Not the old
ones, with the fading paint and the bubbly engine whine. The
new ones. Brightly colored, with a matching daisy poking up
from a vase stuck in the dash. How horrible to be mowed down
by a happy little car with its own matching, factory-installed
flower. It's undignified.

One night, while eating dinner with Sabrina and my mother,
I throw out the question: What car would you least like to be
killed by? In return, I get only blank stares. "You think I'm
being ridiculous, but it could happen. Look around the next
time you're driving. Nobody is paying attention. They're on the
phone or rubbernecking or arguing. They're singing, eating—
hell, roadhead is a thing that happens."

My mother isn't amused.

The third sign comes while I'm lending my friend John a
postmortem hand. John's death came as a surprise but not a
shock. He'd been sick for a while, and what started as a cold
became pneumonia, and from there it all happened very quickly.
He stopped going to work, then stopped answering his door,
and one day he died. Or rather, one day we learned he was dead.
He was home alone when he collapsed. He rotted for a week
before anyone found him. That John died alone and remained
there for seven days is tough to hear. I'm still reeling when the
question comes: Someone has to go in there, open some windows, let out the stink of decomposition. Will I do it?

When I arrive, a neighbor is there with a key to the back
door. He hands it to me almost apologetically and gets back into

his car. As soon as I walk in, I see exactly where John fell. A body left untended for a few days leaves marks—if not indelible, then at least unmistakable. The floor is stained by the brown smudge of decomposition.

There's a long list of the things John was. An unrepentant gunslinger who nearly shot himself twirling a .38. A practical joker who once convinced Ted Turner that he was the spokesman for a Native American group planning to protest Braves games. A recognized genius who abandoned his career at one of Atlanta's most prestigious architectural firms to work in a hardware store. Now he's dead. He hasn't passed away or gone to a better place. He simply died in the basement. I wait for revulsion, tears, anything. But nothing comes. A year ago this would've been out of the question. Opening the windows, thumbing through his books, unloading his pistol—it would have been too much. A year ago I would've been outside in the car with my neighbor. Today it's just another call.

Medicine's great magic trick is how it convinces us we're here saving lives when more often what we're doing is witnessing death. Over time, shock wears thin, empathy recedes, and a human being becomes nothing more than something I carry home in the tread of my right boot. This is my new normal, the resting heart rate of my psyche. It's my state of mind as I wonder whether this job's worth it.

My needle stick happened the way they all do. I was distracted, looked away, let my focus drift, and—

"Shit."

I looked down and saw a small hole in the ring finger of my

right glove. I yanked it off, and there, below the middle knuckle, was a tiny pinprick. A red dot of blood.

"Shitshitshitshitshitshitshitshit."

I staggered out of the ambulance. We had no hand sanitizer, only sterilizing wipes with a label that warned against using them on babies, food, and bare skin. I scrubbed my finger raw. At the hospital the nurses all looked at me sadly, apologetically. They'd talk to the patient, talk to the administration, gain access to her records, and get permission to test her.

"Test for what?"

"To see if she has, well, you know . . . AIDS."

My knees wobbled.

One of the nurses pulled me aside, said she'd been there, knew what it felt like. "Of course," she said, "my patient was an old woman. Thank God. I knew right away she didn't have anything. But still . . ."

My boss was cavalier. He drove me to get my blood drawn, then dropped me off at the station so I could get my car. Someone else was already on my ambulance, already running my calls. By now, everyone knew why. I wasn't even dead, and already my obituary had been written. My boss said he'd call me with updates on the patient: It turned out they couldn't force her to submit to a blood test, she had to agree to one. If she didn't, they could take her to court, but who knew how long that would take. Either way, I couldn't work until my results came back. "Go home," he said. "Relax, whatever." I got out. He unrolled his window, leaned out. "If you bang your wife tonight? Make sure you double-bag it."

Sabrina wanted to know who it was. What kind of person. I told her it was a twenty-two-year-old who lived in a project and was pregnant for the fifth time. Sabrina slumped onto the couch, half-mad, half-grief-stricken.

I've spent three long days waiting and the results are in. A receptionist calls me back. She leads me through the swinging double doors and into the main treatment center. We pass through a small clinic—me breathless, her shuffling along—and then through another set of doors, and everything goes quiet. This is an old wing of an old building, all but forgotten by everyone except those called back here to have their fortunes read. There are posters on the walls, PSAs about drugs and premarital sex, teen pregnancy, sexually transmitted diseases. My heart is pounding so hard that my gums start to tingle. I'm seeing spots, sweating, a little nauseous. The joints in my knees loosen, so I'm not walking as much as jangling, and right about then the floor drops out from under me. The receptionist speaks, but her words come from somewhere deep under the surface of a pool.

I'm sitting in a tiny office of Sheetrock walls. The filing cabinets are overstuffed, the metal-frame desk is crowded with stacks of folders. Behind it, opposite me, is a guy in his thirties with dreads and a soft smile. He's holding a file, my file, and he asks me—the words in slow motion at first but picking up speed—if I have any questions. *Yes, I have questions. What the fuck do you think? My results. I want to know my results.*

"Oh. Fine. All good. They didn't tell you over the phone?"

"No."

Turns out I'm clean, as is the patient. She's had so many children spread out over so many years that the hospital has an ongoing record of her medical history. Every birth, every illness, every hiccup. Not one communicable disease has ever been found.

I let out a sigh of relief and a small grateful laugh at having been sentenced to death only to receive a last-second pardon.

As for whether the job is worth it, I have only this. When I leave, I make two calls—the first is to Sabrina, saying I'm okay. The second is to my supervisor, asking him to put me back on the schedule.

19

The Perfect Call

It's my first shift back, and Chris and I have been dispatched to a pedestrian hit by a car. He's facedown when we find him, dead in front of Red Lobster. Even as we're pronouncing him, a cop lazily strings yellow police tape around us. It's dark, and people have begun to wander over, but the crowd isn't big yet—not pushing on the tape, straining to catch a glimpse.

In the relative peace, we have time to stop and consider the dead man's teeth, which have come out—like fleshy dentures— nearly in one piece. How this could happen, I have no clue. It's just one of those inexplicable things that happen when something big and heavy and fast slams into your fleshy parts. There's nothing for us to do here, so I'm heading for the ambulance when I see a flash go off behind me. I turn. Chris has the camera in his hand, and he seems almost surprised. He looks at me, the body, the camera. Neither of us says a word, but the message is clear: We've spent so much time looking for carnage and taking pictures of oddities that the two have merged. He hasn't taken a picture of the body, just the teeth—perfect and disembodied, lying in the road like a windup gag toy. What would we even do with such a picture?

No time to think. Our radios light up again.

Our lights flash red off the passing buildings. The strobes flicker in the night. Chris is speeding. The dispatcher's voice crackles over the radio. A high school dance has just let out, and all hell's breaking loose. When the call first comes, it's for a single person shot, but they're still shooting and the number increases to two. Then three. We get there almost before the shooting stops.

We park, get out, and take in the scene—dozens of panicked students screaming, dozens more pulling up in cars, a gas station attendant locking his doors, police trying unsuccessfully to cordon off the area, a news helicopter already buzzing on the horizon, and in the middle of it all, three patients, *our* patients, bleeding and alone. We grab our bag but leave the stretcher. With each step, we crunch spent shell casings—cops are reporting over ninety shots fired, a number that doesn't seem possible.

When we reach our patients, two are standing and one is sitting quietly on the ground. There's a tall kid, nervous and jangly, who's been shot through the right shoulder and left leg. Next to him is a kid who took one bullet through the tip of his nose and another through his upper lip; that bullet passed through his teeth and lodged in his hard palate. He doesn't say a word, just stares at us with big open eyes. The third patient is a big mass of childhood obesity who's been shot through the arm. He's the calmest, the least critical, and nods to each of our questions. We call him the Buddha.

We're waiting for a second unit, but the scene is an absolute madhouse. A fire crew has arrived, and they're panicking—one of them steps on the Buddha, and the captain, who never gets closer than five feet, keeps screaming pointlessly into his radio for a transport helicopter. High school kids are arriving by the carload, each group more agitated than the last. A second news helicopter arrives, procreates with the first, and together they give birth to a dozen more. And then there's the recurring ghost story, yelled every few seconds, that the shooters, whoever they are, have come back. Each time it sends waves of panic through the crowd. The scene is loud, hot, messy, and stinks of gasoline and blood. Bystanders are screaming, our patients are screaming, the fire captain—"Where is my damn medevac!"—is screaming.

"Fuck it," Chris says. "Let's take 'em all."

"All three? You wanna take all three?"

"You're right," he says. "Let's take two. Which one you wanna leave?"

Thirty seconds later, we have everyone loaded into the ambulance. The tall one can't shut his mouth, and the kid shot in the face can't be still. The Buddha sits quietly on the end of the bench. Chris nods to me, and I jump up front and roar off. All told, we're on-scene fewer than seven minutes. Chris bounces off the walls as he struggles to cut off clothes, bandage, start IVs, call the hospital, and reassess. When we arrive, I jump out and grab a passing medic, who helps us wagon-train the three of them through the triage area and straight back to the trauma rooms. The whole world is waiting for us back there, and it's nothing but blinding lights and questions, nurses, doctors, phlebotomists, x-ray techs, registration clerks, surgeons. Cops trail in behind us, asking their own questions. Clear bags with twine drawstrings are filled with clothes, wallets, watches, rings, necklaces, phones, belts, shoes, and—

"What's this?"

Even in the midst of the chaos, the noise, the rising panic
from the kid shot twice in the face, there's something in the
tone—the suggestion of a problem—that catches my attention. I turn to see a doctor looking at the Buddha's lower back,
a gloved hand pressing him forward. Chris is looking, too, the
color drained from his face. The doctor looks up, calls out a
single entrance wound four inches right of the spine, lower
back—right in the kidney. No exit.

Usually, in the immediate aftermath of a shit-kicker, the
sudden quiet only amplifies all the leftover adrenaline. It hits
like a head full of meth, and I'm high, almost bouncing, as the
details sort themselves out and, for the first time since arriving
on-scene, I have a chance to think about what I've just done.
This moment and the memory of it, the promise that others like
it are out there somewhere, waiting, are what keep me going
through the dry spells when we run nothing but headaches and
angry, piss-covered drunks. But tonight we can't enjoy it. We're
frustrated and rattled. Out on the ramp, our ambulance is nothing but blood, bandages, and discarded packaging. The two-way
radio dangles by its cord, smudged with bloody fingerprints. I
lean in, look to where the Buddha was seated, and there on the
wall, at kidney height, is a splotch of blood.

That we'd missed it isn't totally shocking. We had three
patients fall into our lap, and our scene time was seven minutes; major trauma allows for ten minutes. It was hectic, we
were outgunned. A lacerated kidney—if that's what the wound
ends up being—is a problem for the surgeons; there's nothing
we would've done differently had we noticed it. But we didn't
notice it, and that's the point. It isn't that we could have saved
him or bettered his care or had the hospital more prepared.

This is a matter of pride. We got our wish. We got our call—or something as close to it as possible—and we were less than perfect.

We drive back in a funk. We drop the camera off at CVS, which is open twenty-four hours and manned by a dirty little creature who clearly won't be scandalized by the photo of the teeth. After the film spins through the machine, the pictures are printed and slipped into an envelope. Outside, Chris riffles through, finds the shot of the teeth, tears it up, and throws it away. We ordered doubles, so I get my own set of what was on the roll. By the next morning, we've shaken it off. We both agree the call was fun, that it went well, that certain allowances can be made for the fog of war. As for the picture, we don't talk about it.

When I get home, I shower. Afterward, hair wet, half-dressed, I pull out the photos and thumb through. And there, staring up at me from the top of the stack, is the picture. The teeth, slick with blood, whole and accusatory. Like a thief through the window or a rat through the crawlspace, they have violated my home. I quickly throw away the photo but can't escape the fact that it's in my house. I tear it up, but it's still there. Finally, I burn it. It's gone, but like on the wall behind the Buddha's seat, the stain remains.

A few shifts later, Chris gets fired. Not because of the teeth or even the Buddha. It's about T-shirts. Fucking T-shirts. Chris had printed out shirts—with the logos of both Rural/Metro and Fulton County Fire—and sold them for ten dollars apiece, not to the general public but to us. We all bought them, we all wore them. Some firefighter who never liked Chris complained and carried his grievance higher and higher up in the chain until a fire chief and some suit from Rural/Metro got together and agreed that Chris had reproduced their respective logos without proper authorization. And so a damn good medic got fired for a copyright violation. This is how the world comes undone.

20

Rules to Live By

Chris's firing ends my brief stint as a True Believer. What happened is proof that pettiness can exist even in the midst of extraordinary circumstances. I still love the job, but never again will I be so seduced. I complain nightly to Sabrina, who has no patience for it. We agree it's time for a change. The only thing stopping me from resigning from Rural/Metro right now and applying to Grady is paramedic school. The class, sponsored by Fulton County, is specifically tailored to our peculiar twenty-four on/forty-eight off work schedule. I'll be done in three months, so I vow to sit tight, keep my head down, and finish. The second I get my numbers, I'm out.

As for paramedic school, it's okay. It's longer and more rigorous than EMT school, and we learn dozens of drugs and procedures—how to intubate, read a cardiac monitor, deliver shocks, and treat a sucking chest wound. We're supposed to spend hundreds of hours doing clinicals, shadowing doctors in ERs and ORs and on the OB floor, and many more riding third on ambulances. All this while working. I skip the clinicals and fudge my paperwork—so much for heroes. But the classwork is fairly demanding. We start with sixty, maybe seventy students. We finish with a dozen.

The months pass in a blur. I wake up at the station, head throbbing from only two hours of sleep, and go straight to class in the uniform I wore the night before. Brush my teeth in the bathroom down the hall. Then sit and learn about the heart, the lungs, the brain. Why the kidneys fail and what happens when they do. The endocrine system, pediatrics. For most people, it's enough to learn the signs and symptoms, the indicators of disease processes that are at the root of why your father is unconscious on the floor. As for me . . . lately, I've begun to see signs that the Tourist is back. I've tried to ignore it, study harder, work more. But I can no longer deny it.

Today we're watching autopsies, something I've been looking forward to for months. When we arrived at class this morning, instead of settling in for a lecture, we piled into a half-dozen cars and drove to the Georgia Bureau of Investigation. We're now gathered in a conference room, waiting. Finally, an investigator walks in, smiles, and asks if anyone's squeamish. "I know you've all seen the dead," she explains when we laugh. "But here, in an autopsy, you don't merely *see* a dead body. You *dissect* it."

The staff cuts up three bodies while we watch.

The first is a man who drowned in a lake on his birthday and whose waterlogged nuts poke up into the air like a cantaloupe. Next is a man who ran over a bee's nest while mowing. Rather than go for help, he panicked and locked himself in the bathroom. Last is a woman who had a heart attack in a grocery store. I look around. All my classmates are marveling at the cross-sectioned heart, eyes wide with wonder as the medical examiner shows us the offending lump of goop that broke free, stopped up her left anterior descending artery, and killed her instantly. They're mesmerized, and all I can think about is the cart full of groceries—her uneaten last meal—that had to be solemnly re-stocked by a fifteen-year-old making minimum wage. What must *that* have been like? Forget the heart, the blockage, the anatomy of this woman's death. I want to talk to the grocery clerk.

The day before my paramedic exam, I have breakfast with Chris. Though he's working somewhere else, we get together on occa-sion. I'm nervous about the exam, but he says I'm ready. Or as ready as I'm gonna be. He says the first six months will be the hardest. "You won't know what you're doing, and you'll fuck things up, but probably not so bad anybody dies."

"You sure about that?"

"Yup."

Then he gives me three pieces of advice that he counts off on his fingers, starting with his thumb. "One: Know your proto-cols. Two: Don't second-guess yourself. Three: Never let 'em see you sweat." These should be my *rules,* he says. I should commit them to memory, hold on to them, live by them, call on them in moments of crisis when all hell is breaking loose.

Despite Chris's stamp of approval, I'm nervous. The minute I pass this exam, I'm a medic. That means I'll no longer be an observer or an assistant. I'll be the one whose decisions determine the outcome of a stranger's emergency. Forget the medicine, for-get the extra twelve months of classes—what separates paramedic school from EMT school is that getting through and becoming a medic means accepting the mantle of final responsibility.

When I'm a medic, it will all come down to me.

BOOK THREE

Top of the World

21

Do No (Serious) Harm

A man stabs a woman in the chest. He does it with a dull pocketknife, rusted and grimy from a decade spent in his pants pocket. She screams and staggers backward, trailing blood through a crack house that's beyond filthy, urban decay taken to a hellish extreme. To the junkies and dealers, this place is home. To the neighborhood's elderly and infirm—poverty's hostages—it's a haunted house. Windows broken or missing. Door long since kicked in. Water leaking through the roof that warps the floors and turns the plaster walls into mush. A toilet no longer connected to the outside world, filled and overflowing with unimaginable waste. A rotating cast of crackheads turned genderless by desperation, who, with their lips blistered from white-hot crack pipes, give five-dollar blow jobs.

So what if a woman is stabbed in the chest? It's just another day in the Zoo.

This is the first call I run after upgrading from EMT to medic. My first call working for Grady. I'm sitting in the passenger seat, uniform too new to fit right, with a studied look of nonchalance. The day the notice arrived in the mail that I'd passed my paramedic exam, I applied at Grady. As luck would have it, they were hiring. I underwent a physical, a written test, and a practical evaluation, smiled through an interview, then deposited my sign-on bonus. We spent three weeks in a classroom learning the Grady Way, then another three with field training officers, putting it into practice. Now I'm speeding through the streets, trying to focus but unable to think through the siren's scream. We're in the Bluff—the very part of town that Pike railed about three years ago during my ride-alongs—on our way to a crack house known as the Zoo, a place so notorious that someone has taken the time to spray-paint the words over the missing front door. As Biggie once said, if you don't know, now you know.

We pull up on-scene and walk through the house, but the patient is no longer here. We find her a block away, shirtless and screaming, fingers crack-burned, lips crack-burned, pants wet from God knows what. She has a red flower of flesh bursting out from her left breast. I try to listen to her lungs—ostensibly to see how far the knife has penetrated into the chest wall, and whether her chest cavity is filling with air or blood. In reality, I just need something to do. My hands tremble, my heart flutters, there's a weakness in my stomach. I listen but hear nothing. Which could be bad. It could also be that we're surrounded by noises: the distant whirl of a siren, the scream of the patient, the insistent yelling of the bystanders, the shouts of the drug dealers as they warn each other of approaching cops.

I'm starting to panic. I run through Chris's list of rules and land on "Never let 'em see you sweat." I take a deep breath, followed by a longer exhale. It's not helping. The patient is still screaming. My partner is waiting for direction, but not for long. If I don't make a decision and set the chain of events into motion, she'll begin to act on her own, and there's no recovering from that. The call will be out of sequence, and worse, when it's over, word will spread that I froze. To nut up, as they call it, is an act of paralysis, and it would leave an indelible black smudge on my reputation. No one would want to work with me, and those forced to would never trust me. All of this is in danger of happening, seems *destined* to happen, when—without warning, without provocation—the patient turns and runs. Disappears between two houses. I look at my partner, and she looks at me. Before either of us can say a word, a cop walks up behind us and says, "Did you see the tits on that broad?"

The day Chris passed down to me those three rules, he also gave me his clipboard. It's the clipboard we carried with us on every call, through every house, every situation we went through. It was the dented reminder of the confidence I'd built and the experience I'd gained in our time together. After he gave it to me I turned it in my hands, felt its heft. I opened it and took out the patient pen. Chris yanked on the end, and it farted. We both laughed.

Months later, I'm laughing once again—this time with a cop I don't know and at a patient who's all mine. As we stand in the street watching the patient—shirtless, pendulous breasts swinging in the heat—run in and out of view, I add a fourth rule: Look for the weird and take time to laugh. My mind has been so crowded with the practicalities of medicine that I've forgotten why I'm here in the first place. And it's this. So I can stand in the street and witness this moment. I smile. I laugh. My hands stop trembling. I motion for the cop to go one way around the house and for my partner to go the other. They flush her out, and I'm waiting. She's still yelling, and it occurs to me that it's not only unlikely but impossible to scream with your lungs punctured and filling with blood. This isn't serious. We take her to the ambulance and away from the chaos. She stops yelling but keeps talking. Still alive, still panicking, still very high on crack.

We do a quick assessment, and it turns out she was only stabbed in the boob. Still, it looks nasty. The human body— hers, mine, everyone's—is basically sausage. Puncture the skin, really puncture it, and fatty tissue explodes out like a pink mushroom cloud. It stays that way, wobbling like chewed bubble gum, until it's stuffed back in and the hole is closed. It's neither practical nor hygienic to do this in an ambulance. I would never get the wound clean enough and in the end she'd wind up with a big festering boob. Which really isn't ideal. So I put a clean dressing on it while the cop tries to figure out what happened. The conversation loops around and around until it comes out that her boyfriend caught her smoking his crack, and well, the rest we know. The boyfriend's name is Fat-Fat, and the victim doesn't want to press charges. The cop hops out and closes the door. My partner puts the truck in gear, and we roll away.

When it's all over, my partner and I laugh and then run more calls. She's unaware how close I was to coming unglued, how close she was to issuing my death sentence by telling everyone that I'm no good.

It continues like this day after day, calls coming in and me on the very edge of panic. It's only a matter of time before the Big One shows up. Every new medic knows his first real test is out there, so I wait—half dreading it, half breathless with anticipation. When other medics speak, I hang on every word, peppering them with questions. I try to be discreet, but my desperation shows. *What did you do? How'd you know to do that? What were the signs? Had you seen someone catch on fire before, or was the treatment something you learned in school?* I'm looking for answers or help or peace of mind—an indication that I'll be able to handle the moment when it's my turn. I casually solicit tips and advice, anything that'll tell me what I should already know, what I'm paid to know. For my peers, we're talking shop and telling war stories. Everyone else is looking for a laugh; I'm looking for advice.

Then one day it arrives. My first real test comes without warning, as just another call, though it's not. This stranger, the one whose death will fall in my lap, appears from nowhere to read my fortune and decide whether my future holds a transfer to a quiet fire service or a decade of riding out the madness on an ambulance.

My partner and I are sitting around talking when the call comes in. Our radio crackles with static and then the words— *person shot, multiple wounds.* My skin goes cold. She's twenty- nine, and she's been shot six times at close range. What that is—being shot six times at close range—is beyond malice or anger. It's pure hate. It's death by a loved one. It happens on the far edge of town.

We're a long way out when the dispatch comes in, and with traffic, we're slow to arrive. I hop out of the truck, and even from here I can see her, floating in a thick pool of blood that's congealed into red pudding. The crowd is screaming, all emo- tion and panic. They know the victim and the perp, they know the police can't control them. Over the shouting, I hear the patient gurgling through blood and clenched teeth. This is the real thing. Someone has been shot but not killed, and now I'm here, alone, to deal with it. My partner is competent but new, and just an EMT, so it's all on me. No one to fall back on, no one to help, no time to think. The patient, my patient, is dying.

We lower the stretcher. She's nothing but holes, blood, and a pair of brown eyes locked to the right and staring at a serious brain bleed. Someone is screaming for everyone to back up, to stop touching us, to give us room. I think it's my partner, but it could be me. It's hard to say. My brain's in a blender. I suction the patient's mouth, watch blood swirl up the tubing. Then we strap her to a backboard and the stretcher's up and moving. More suctioning. In the ambulance, air conditioner's blowing warm air. Counting holes. Ventilating. Suctioning. Finding more holes. An IV in each arm. Fluids. Lots of fluids. A call to the hospital interrupted by a seizure. Enough seizure-stopping Versed to put down a horse. Finally, serenity.

Right before we get to the hospital, I do a final count for holes. Three in her chest, one in the neck, one in the face. I've slipped a hand under her head to check for head shots when her eyes pop open. I let go. Her eyes close. I press again. Her eyes pop open. There's a firefighter riding with us, and we look at each other as it becomes clear: My finger has slipped through a bullet hole and into her skull, and whatever I'm poking in there is making her eyes open and close. I say that's probably not good, and he nods. "No, I don't think that's good."

"I'm not gonna do that again."

"Probably best."

At the hospital, she's quickly assessed, further sedated, intubated, and taken to surgery.

The woman dies a little while later, though her boyfriend—barricaded in his apartment—hangs on for a few more hours. We clean the truck, restock what we used, and go back in service. We run more calls. I'm not good yet, but I can lay to rest the question of whether I'll panic when the Big One comes. I am and always will be a Grady medic.

22

The Private Life of a Public Hospital

Grady isn't a hospital. It's a trauma center and a stroke center, a burn unit, a psychiatric facility, an enormous public resource. It's a creaking bureaucracy, underfunded, overburdened, and struggling to pay its bills. Its campus is dotted with clinics and sprawls across an immodest number of city blocks in downtown Atlanta. So it's a hospital, yes. But it's more than that.

Grady is an ecosystem. Swirling around it at all hours of the night are creatures from every level of the food chain. There's a woman who lives in the bus enclosure out front and sings at the top of her lungs. She's not singing songs but hymns, and when we arrive in the morning, we aren't merely punching in to work—we're receiving communion. Out in the streets, just beyond Grady's front doors, are ambulances, doctors, nurses, visitors, the homeless, half-medicated lunatics and patients who've dragged their IV poles outside to smoke. Huddled together on the sidewalks—which are dotted with chewing gum and droplets of blood and the occasional human turd—are anxious family circles praying for loved ones, and the local news reporter who's camped out because something tragic has happened. Something tragic always happens.

There's a McDonald's beneath the parking deck. Hospital

trash is taken out a few yards from the ramp where ambulances bring patients in. This ramp is new. The old one was smaller and faced a different direction and was bordered on one side by a wall. Regulars—vagrants and homeless and down-on-their-luck locals—would sit on the wall and smoke cigarettes. Every time an ambulance came in, they'd clap and cheer. That wall became known as the Rooter Wall, the people perched on its ledge Rooters. To this day, patients transported repeatedly to Grady are called Rooters, and everyone who works here walks a fine line between love and hate when it comes to Rooters.

All this before we get inside.

Grady was built in 1892, and the original building still stands. The main hospital is much newer and infinitely larger and was once segregated into two facilities: one for whites, the other for blacks. Jim Crow is gone but not by much, and poor blacks, ever mindful of their separate-but-equal past, still refer to the hospital—the place they were born, where they're healed, and eventually, where they'll die—as the Gradys.

There's a main entrance with an atrium—marble floors and high ceilings, a receptionist, mounted plaques—but anyone sick, anyone coming by ambulance, enters through triage. Triage is a three-ring circus, and its main attraction is the human body gone suddenly, maybe irrevocably, wrong. Triage is run by two nurses, and at any given time it's occupied by a couple dozen patients in various states of need. The main floor is home to the waiting room and its hundreds of souls in limbo. It's also home to the ECC—what you'd call the ER. The Red Zone houses trauma; the Blue Zone houses medical. Both have a couple dozen rooms, plus twice as many informal hall spots where patients end up, despite having been shot, because someone has confirmed the wound isn't life-threatening. The Red Zone includes the trauma bays where the most critically injured are treated. It's also home to Red Obs, which is a cramped parking lot for violent psych patients too sedated or too in need of medical help to head upstairs.

The Blue Zone has no trauma bays, but it has the CPR room, four critical-care rooms, an asthma room, and the hospital's detention area. Prisoners from the city or county jail, the men locked up in the federal penitentiary, all get handcuffed to a bed and brought to detention.

The ECC is a wild place overflowing with patients, competitive doctors, overworked nurses, and a ballooning coterie of support staff. It was built in the nineties, designed to replace an ER that took the worst the city had to offer, that functioned with a chaotic precision and whose tile walls sported a handful of bullet holes until it was demolished.

The cafeteria is on the second floor; labor and delivery is on the fourth. Every time a baby is born—a child known from that moment on as a Grady Baby—a lullaby is played over the hospital's PA system so everyone knows another life has entered the world. This city has a lot of Grady Babies, thousands, and the song has announced the arrival of so many for so long that halfway through, it fades and hiccups only to gain strength toward the end.

The morgue is in the basement. The psych ward is on thirteen.

Grady is a strange place and very much a part of this city's fabric. The EMS department is no different. Wearing a Grady uniform, driving a Grady ambulance, gets me into and (more important) *out of* countless dangerous situations. People walking

down the street, all of them Rooters, many of them Grady Babies, stop and wave as we drive by. *Hey there, Grady* is yelled
every day from every frayed corner of this city. But it's not
easy. The call volume is enormous—over a hundred thousand
a year—and the patients (mostly homeless, many drunk) are a
handful. Turnover's so high that people who've been around a
while won't speak to me until I've made it six months. That's the
first threshold. If I haven't been fired or quit or killed by then,
I'll probably make it. In the meantime, they ignore me.

Outside of work, on the street and among friends, it's different. The minute I say I work for Grady, I have everyone's attention. The place is so revered, so feared, so mythologized that
saying I work here gets the same reaction every time: *I bet you see
some crazy shit.*

And I do. I've treated a woman stabbed by a stingray at the
aquarium. I've run calls on football players, washed-up actors,
and hysterical strippers. I've been called out to the projects,
the Capitol building, the high-rises, the highway, the jails and
churches, even Tent City—a squatters' refuge on the edge of
town. The hospital itself, yeah, it's crazy, too. In some ways,
a little *too* crazy. Like right now, for instance. I'm sitting in a
small auditorium on the edge of campus listening to a speech on
booby traps. Nobody's sure who's setting them or why, but we all
agree the perpetrator needs to die. Slowly. Painfully.

Every few weeks another booby trap shows up. Maybe it's
a dirty needle, uncapped and taped to the bottom of a seat.
Maybe the needle has been stuck through the foam blocks we
use to immobilize patients. Maybe it's poking out from under
the hood. Today we're listening to an administrator who has
placed a picture on the overhead projector. He flicks it on, and

the image—projected onto a screen at a terrifying twelve feet by twelve feet—is of a plastic bag filled with piss and bristling with uncapped needles. "This was found in an ambulance yesterday," he says. "It was just sitting there in an overhead compartment." He keeps talking but we care about only one thing—who's doing it? He doesn't know. Doesn't want to speculate, isn't here to talk about that. He's telling us to be careful, to check our ambulances carefully. To police ourselves. This isn't what we want to hear. Someone's already been stuck, so no, we don't want to hear that we can minimize our chance of exposure by showing up early and double-checking the truck. We want to hear that the fucker's been caught, that he's tied up outside for us to look at: *Here he is, guys! Take a swing.* Instead, someone has left a bag of piss needles in an ambulance, and we're told to police ourselves. I can't even answer the why of such a situation, let alone speculate on the who. "Okay," he says, snapping off the overhead projector and slipping the photo back into a manila folder. "That's all I have."

We file out of the room and, despite our reservations, clock in. We grab our equipment and head out to the ramp. We enter our ambulances very, very slowly.

23

There's Been a Prison Break

Still, I love it here. Forget the booby traps and anonymous ter-rorists, the plastic bags full of piss and needles. Grady is the only place I want to be. It's nothing but history and controversy, and its medics—all those people who won't speak to me—are the best around. I want desperately to earn their respect. I thought the shooting would do it—that maybe people would notice how I sped to the far end of town for a woman shot too many times at too close a range to be anything but an organ donor. How I stayed calm, did my job, and delivered her in better shape than I found her. But it was just one call among a hundred thousand, and I'm just one among two dozen new guys. Nobody noticed and nobody knows my name. Not the other medics and cer-tainly not the director of operations.

Until now.

It's dark outside, not even seven in the morning, and I'm standing before the director of EMS operations. She runs our department, and until this morning she'd had neither a reason nor the time to form an opinion of me. Now she's considering my future. This isn't good. It's been three years since I got into EMS. In that time, I worked my way onto a 911 ambulance, graduated from paramedic school, and got hired at the only place I've ever wanted to work EMS. There are harder paths, but this one's mine. Or was, anyway. It's hard to say what'll happen from here.

The director is stone-faced and serious, because the charges—and people *are* threatening charges—have gotten serious. She wants to know what in hell I was thinking, but I have no answer. I fidget. My eyes flick around the room as I try to imagine what I'll say to Sabrina when I call. That I've been fired? That I've been arrested? That things are about to change because I couldn't keep my hands off the radio?

"I'm going to make this simple," she says, hands pressed flat against her desk. "Tell me *exactly* what you said. Word for word." She holds up a written complaint. "Because this? It doesn't make sense."

"I mean, all I said, really, it was only two words." I'm stammering, hands up in a defensive posture. "Unless you want to be technical, because *technically*, it was eighteen words. Give or take."

Her mouth slips open like she's forgotten it's there.

I clear my throat. "See, it was, um, it was Sunday morning. And you know how those are."

Of course she knows. We all know. Sundays are easy. Working a Sunday is a gift to EMS. A small thank-you for the long hours, for carrying fat people down stairs, for stepping in the still-warm turd your patient dropped in the hallway, and what's more, for never mentioning it. Sundays are a reward for remaining calm despite being outgunned and remaining on duty despite residing—permanently—on the lowest rung of the caregiver pay scale. Sundays are relaxing, and so long as nobody dies in church, Sunday is a good day. But Sunday can also be boring.

Most of us are at Grady because Grady is always busy. We never stop, we're up in the middle of it all—the city, the trauma, the excitement, everything. Until Sunday. When it gets slow. And there's nothing but the quiet of a phone that never rings, the boredom of a call that isn't dispatched. Time stretches on forever. And we wait.

And wait.

And waiting isn't necessarily a good thing for someone who's wired to never stop moving. They say idle hands are the devil's workshop, but what they don't say is when it comes time to explain yourself, the devil's never around to help. So I'm alone, explaining the inexplicable, and basically, the story goes like this.

The day it all happens, I'm working an eight-hour overtime shift. I'm paired with an EMT I get along with, so right from the start, we're in a good mood. When we go in-service, dispatch sends us to the southeastern corner of the city. There's nothing down here but a handful of housing projects and some rowdy apartments, but it's early when we roll in, and it'll be a few hours before they get out of bed and start acting up. We park across the street from the federal penitentiary.

Forget the barbed wire and guard towers, the searchlights, the guns, the unspeakable past of its inmates, and Atlanta's federal pen isn't menacing. It was built in 1902 and has a precise, austere beauty. From our spot across the street, it looks less like the onetime home of Al Capone than a branch of the Federal Reserve. We sit for a while in silence. The stereo doesn't work, and the gas station doesn't have any newspapers. We talk until we run out of things to say and then, almost absentmindedly, I pick up the radio mike. Some of the newer trucks don't have this feature, but on the older ones, there's a switch that turns the radio into a PA. Flip it to radio and I'm talking to the dispatcher. Flip it to PA and I'm talking to the world. I don't have a plan, this isn't thought out, and I have no intention of making a statement. I just flip it on. Key up and let go, key up and let go, sending little metallic clicks out into the morning.

After a few minutes, I key up and whisper a long and dreamy hello. At the beginning, everything seems innocent, so we keep it up—whispering, singing, issuing commands in a heavy, almost indecipherable Scottish accent. When this, too, gets boring, we set it down. But no calls come out, and there's nothing to do, and it's just sitting there, waiting. What harm could possibly come from going back one more time? I switch the radio back to PA and key up the mike. The speaker clicks on and I pause, broadcasting dead air and my own breath out into the neighborhood. And then—on a quiet Sunday morning not even a block away from the federal penitentiary—I tell everyone within earshot the worst has happened.

"May I have your attention, please? There has been a jailbreak. I repeat, there has been a jailbreak."

For a few seconds nothing happens. There's no panic. No stampede. No sign at all that anyone has heard us. And then, across the street, a door opens. A skinny little hipster bolts out onto his porch. At first I don't pay him any mind. It's eight in the morning, we're in a bad neighborhood, and this guy's got a pirate flag hanging from his house. I don't see him as the type who wants to be taken seriously. I'm wrong.

He darts down the steps and stomps barefoot across the street. We pretend not to see him even as we watch him march over. "He headed our way?" I ask, mouth barely moving. My partner nods, turns off the PA. This should be fun. The guy stomps up to the driver's-side window and starts yelling. No hello, no nothing. Yelling. My partner, God bless him, smiles through the glass. He holds a hand to his ear and says, "I can't hear you."

This infuriates the little guy. "Unroll it, then!"

My partner reaches up and presses the window button, slowly lowering the window with a loud, rubbery squuuueeee-aaaaakkkk. He smiles. "What's up?"

The guy rails on for five minutes, mostly about us waking him up at eight on a Sunday morning but with a heavy emphasis on the fact that people live here. He says he's heard everything we've said, every word, from his house across the street. I ask, because I can't help myself, which house is his. "The one with the pirate flag?"

His hair catches fire.

He opens his mouth, then stops. He turns and marches off, and right about then my partner and I decide it's a good time to leave. We don't make it half a block before we catch a call. We flick on the lights and head over, and almost immediately, we forget about the hipster, the PA, even the jailbreak. But the hipster remembers us. Before we leave the scene of our call, a white supervisor's truck pulls up. The supervisor gets out and walks over. He asks if we had an argument with a resident. I nod. "Yeah, some guy over by the prison. Why?"

"Did you say something about a jailbreak?"

It occurs to me, for the first time and clearly too late, that while sitting in an official-looking vehicle, I'd announced there'd been a jailbreak. Over a PA system. A block from the federal penitentiary. This was probably a bad idea.

The supervisor pulls his keys from his pocket. "After you guys drop that patient off," he says, hopping into his truck, "go ahead and come by my office. We need to talk."

It's a very long transport.

As soon as we walk through the door, our supervisor drops it on us. "He wants to press charges."

I've been standing, but once this is said, I sink down into a chair. While we were out running that last call, the hipster went ape shit and called every number he could find, all the way up to the CEO of the hospital. Thankfully, it's a Sunday, and the only person he could get is the supervisor sitting before us. Not that he's terribly happy with us at the moment.

"Reckless endangerment." The supervisor slips his glasses on, reads from a notepad. "He thinks what you said, coming from a city truck, near the pen, was official enough to make it like yelling *fire* in a crowded theater."

I'm in disbelief. "Is he serious?"

"He wants you arrested."

"That's pretty serious."

"I'd say so."

"What now?"

The supervisor shrugs. Says for us to go about the rest of our day like nothing's happened. "What'll happen tomorrow, when everyone returns, I don't know."

That's the story, and what happens now, on Monday, is what I'm here to find out. The director of EMS operations is silent. I clear my throat.

"Look, this was my fault. My partner, he was there, but I said it." I rock back on my heels. "If anyone's getting fired, it should be me."

She nods, which, when you think about it, could mean a

lot of things. She closes her eyes, and we settle into an awkward silence. Then, almost imperceptibly, the bottom corner of her mouth twitches. That's followed by another twitch, then another, and soon her entire mouth breaks out into a huge grin. She tries to regain her composure, to look serious, but it's too late. At last she laughs. I laugh. She cocks her head. I shut up. A deep breath in, a long exhale, and then—

"Did you really say that?"

"Yes, ma'am."

Another smile. "You know you're an idiot, right?"

"That's what my wife says."

"Get back to work. I'll take care of this guy."

"Thank you. Thank you."

Then, as I'm leaving: "Mr. Hazzard?"

"Ma'am?"

"No more PA."

"Done."

So this is how I make my mark, the way people finally learn my name. Not because I ran a tough call and did a commendable job but because I did something stupid. Something funny. Something nobody's ever done. I'm no longer just a newbie. I'm the wiseass who came *this close* to getting arrested.

24

Courage Under Mustard

Seven months at Grady, and I'm already on my third full-time partner. My first month I worked with someone different every shift. It wasn't bad, but I was happy when an EMT was given the spot permanently. Of course, *permanent* is a relative term here at Grady, and after six months he moved on. My next "permanent" partner lasted under a month. This is how it goes here. Grady has so many different shifts—different days, different hours, different lengths—that when we first arrive, everyone's thrashing around in the dark, trying to find something that works. I've gotten lucky with partners so far: nobody burned out or incompetent or all that annoying, even. This last point—that no one's been annoying—is the most important thing. Spending so much time in close quarters with a stranger—no personal space, plenty of pressure—can be bad enough when we get along. But if we don't like each other? Unbearable. So I'm always a little nervous when I show up for the start of a new shift.

My new partner's name is Marty, and we've been working together a few weeks. We'd never met before we started working together. All I knew was that he's a medic, so theoretically, working with him should've made my life easier. I was hopeful, practically excited, that first day. Now . . . not so much. We became partners toward the end of the summer, and from day one the city was jumping. Almost before I knew Marty's name, we were dispatched to a couple of cardiac arrests and a bicyclist hit by a car. We ran some very sick children, a stroke or two, a man found beaten unconscious who had his gold chain but not his wallet, his toupee but not his teeth.

They say the closest bonds are formed in situations of incredible stress, though frankly, that hasn't been the case here. This city has thrown everything it's got at us, and still I'm not sure about Marty. He's not a bad guy, just hard to read. He's younger than I, young enough to have a girlfriend who's in college. This semester she's studying abroad, and in his mind, she's not taking advantage of a great opportunity but *taking a break*. He's always moping, and our interactions are flavored by the indifferent taste of depression—he speaks without making conversation, he laughs without smiling. Until his phone rings. It's *her*, it always is, nobody else calls him. He'll whisper into the phone for twenty minutes, giggling and giddy, only to slip back into a funk the moment she hangs up. When I do get him to talk, it's always about Ohio. People from Ohio are like New Yorkers, always bragging about their hometown, except New Yorkers actually have something to brag about. Marty goes on and on about the Browns, the Indians, Ohio State. He talks about Lebron—my God, he never shuts up about Lebron. He'll also talk about the film *Top Gun*, and worse, he loves rock ballads. Think Air Supply, ELO, and Journey, all sung at a barely audible whisper.

I could look beyond all of this if it weren't for the birds. Because I'm not gonna lie, the bird thing is weird. The first time I noticed it, we were walking through a vacant lot when a car horn startled a couple dozen pigeons. They took flight and were on us, a dirty blanket of fluttering wings. I was annoyed; Marty was terrified. He stood frozen in place, arms locked at his sides, eyes closed, chin tucked to his chest. When I asked about it, he said it was nothing, but after two or three times, he could no longer deny it. "Yes, fine," he yelled. "I'm afraid of birds."

Afraid of birds.

He says the beaks are scary, but what really freaks him out is a bird with an erratic flight pattern. Hawks, with their slow and easy glide? No big deal. But a pigeon? Or a parakeet? *Petrifying.* I laugh. He gets indignant. "It's not that weird."

I disagree. He Googles his particular affliction to prove it's been recognized by the Internet-based medical community. It's called ornithophobia. According to Wikipedia, Scarlett Johansson has it. "It may be irrational," he insists, "but it's real. Says so right there."

So he's afraid of birds. Every day it's the same: strange conversations and small talk, long pauses—the monotony of the jilted psyche—punctuated by the occasional call from Her. This is how it is right now. We're in an ambulance, idling outside a Kmart on Cleveland Avenue. He's whispering into the phone. I'm next to him, silent, pretending not to listen. It's tough, in an ambulance, to give even the appearance of privacy. I stare out the window. The Kmart is a freak show. Bargain hunters arriving in half-dead Mercury Sables, homeless men digging around the trash, hookers limping out of the Palace Inn and across the parking lot in search of more business. Today there's a guy with a pressure washer and a huge drum of water strapped to a trailer hitched to his van. He's set out cones and a sign advertising car washing and hand-detailing. At only fifteen dollars, it seems like a steal.

"Baby girl," Marty whispers into the phone, "I know you're having fun, but at least when the semester's over, you'll be coming back to me." Silence. Then, "Right?"

I press my face to the glass and pretend I'm not here, not listening. I watch a man wander across the parking lot. He walks up to the car washer. They talk for a moment, it's animated like old friends catching up, and then, suddenly, a gunshot. The car washer pulled a gun so fast, I never saw the motion. There was just the pop. Just like that—*POP*—and we've seen a man get shot.

For once it's Marty who ends the call. "I gotta go." He hangs up, phone still to his ear.

For a few seconds nobody moves—the shooter, his victim, Marty, or me—as if none of this is permanent, as if a little quiet will undo what's just been done.

This isn't how it normally goes. Normally, this sort of thing happens near but not close, maybe heard but never seen. The dispatch radio chirps, and a voice comes over the air to say something terrible has happened and could we hurry on over to take a look. Today it's different. Today we've watched it.

Finally, as if insisting his injury is serious, as if to prove he's truly in mortal danger, that he's been shot and not merely insulted, the man staggers back. He puts a hand over his throat, and his knees buckle. Then he starts running.

"Where's he going?"

"He's running."

"Why's he running?"

The man turns, and for an instant it looks like he's running to us.

"Is he running to us? Why's he running to us?"

"Well, this is an ambulance . . ."

Oh.

But he's not running to us. He struggles on at a slow trot, blood streaming down his arm and trickling into the parking lot.

"Now where's he going?"

"Should we follow him?"

"Yeah."

Marty puts the truck in gear and takes his foot off the brake. We start rolling forward, and when we catch up to him, what am I supposed to say? Marty has to remind me to roll my window down. Once it's open, I lean out. "Hey, uh, you wanna get in?"

The guy looks over—eyes bulging, tongue out. Blood runs through his fingers. I don't know how long he can keep this up.

Marty leans over my seat. "You're shot, dude!"

The guy stops, but we keep going, roll right past him like he's nothing but a ghost in the side mirror. Finally, brake lights. The ambulance rocks to a halt. We step out into the parking lot. I've seen plenty of people who've *been* shot, but I haven't seen anyone *get* shot. Until now. This is a whole new experience, and as I grab the patient's arm, I feel a tingle at the base of my spine, evolution's genetic heirloom—someone tried to kill this man, and standing next to him, saving him, I'm prey, too. I look up to see if we're in the crosshairs, but to my shock, the car washer—the shooter—is calmly picking up his buckets and mops. He stacks his cones neatly in a pile, then sits on the bumper and pulls out his phone. Ultimately, it's the shooter who calls 911.

It's curious, really, but there's no time to think about it. We hustle the patient into the back and start driving. This man, it turns out, is lucky beyond measure. The bullet passed through his neck but left his airway and spine intact. He can breathe, he can move, he can talk.

Which is convenient, because the cops meet us at the hospital, and they have questions of their own. Mainly, why the guy who shot him never ran. The patient gives his side of the story—that he was the victim of an attempted robbery. The cops aren't buying it. They ask why a man washing cars in a parking lot would rob a vagrant. And why would he call the police from his own phone and, more, why would he sit calmly on the bumper of his van and wait for the police to arrive?

"I'm the one who got shot!" our patient yells.

One of the cops takes out a pair of handcuffs. "Because you tried to rob him," he says as he cuffs our patient to the bed.

"My word against his."

The cop shakes his head. "The innocent don't run."

Marty and I walk outside. I'm shaking from the adrenaline, giddy from the weirdness. I look to see if Marty's thinking the same thing, to see if he, too, is scared and excited and . . . He's got his eyes closed, chin tucked in. A bird has flown low overhead.

Two shifts later and money is on the line.

"How much are we talking here?"

"To eat the entire bottle of mustard?"

"Yeah."

"Ten dollars."

"Ten dollars."

"Yeah."

"How long do I have?"

Marty thinks he can eat an entire bottle of mustard, start to finish, without stopping. He's so confident that he thinks he can do it now, in the ambulance, while the city crumbles around us. I know he can't, so I want to see him try.

"I think five minutes is fair," I say.

"That doesn't seem like much time. Gimme ten."

"Ten dollars for one bottle of mustard in five minutes."

"Fine."

We drive to a Kroger, and Marty buys a bottle of store-brand stone-ground mustard. He gets a plastic spoon from the deli. We sit in the ambulance and he pours himself a big wobbly spoonful, begins to think this was a bad idea, and eats it. The mustard doesn't go down well. He tries another spoonful, smaller than the first, with more reservation. He chokes it down, takes a deep breath, goes for a third. It gets stuck in his throat.

"Try it without the spoon. Maybe if you can't see it, it won't be so bad."

He tips the bottle to his mouth. Squeezes. Tears run down his cheeks. He shakes his head like a dog that's been dunked in a bath. Drops the bottle on the floor between his feet. "Uh-unh. Nope. Done. I'm done."

I'm driving now, but I'm not watching the road. "You're done?"

"Done."

"Gimme ten bucks."

"Pull over."

"Huh?"

"Pull over."

"Why?"

"I'm gonna puke."

I whip into a gas station. Marty jumps out and throws up in the parking lot. A homeless guy leans against the wall, washing with water from an old two-liter bottle. He stops and watches, his bathwater splashing onto the blacktop. Marty sees him, apologizes. "I'm sorry. I'm sorry. I'm better now. I'm done. Sorry."

The homeless guy resumes washing and Marty pitches forward, hurls again. The homeless guy, disgusted, grabs his stuff and shuffles away. Marty puts a hand up, tries to apologize, to explain, but he can't stop puking.

And here, in the ambulance, I can't stop laughing. Because he's puking, yes. But also because he's publicly and unabashedly making a fool of himself. Because he did something so stupid simply since he thought it'd be funny. I'm laughing because this, at last, is someone I can get along with.

"You okay, Marty?"

"Yup."

"You don't look okay."

"That's because I'm not."

I tell him to take his time, get it all out, I'll wait. As soon as I say this, the dispatcher's voice rings out. "Two-ten," she says over the radio.

I key up the mike. "Go ahead for two-ten."

"I have a call for you."

25

Dead Smurfs

Marty doesn't know anything. Not about how much mustard he can eat and certainly not about this job. He'll be the first to admit it. In fact, that *was* the first thing he admitted when we started working together. As a reminder, he's saying it again now.

"Seriously." He's behind the wheel in his brand-new uniform and untied boots. We've been through this before, but evidently, we need to go through it again. "I don't know anything." He looks at me, serious but unshaken by the admission. "Not a thing."

Marty's saying all this because I haven't been correcting him or guiding him. He reminds me that he and his first partner had what he calls issues. And by *issues,* he means neither of them had any idea what the hell they were doing. That nobody was harmed, killed, or left where they fell because those two couldn't locate the address is pure luck. They knew so little that they couldn't even ask for help—whoever showed up wouldn't have known where to start. So, rather than ask for help, they got lost, got into fights, and treated patients who—miraculously—survived. Eventually, by chance and to the relief of the city's ailing citizens, they got split up. But that's over, and here he is, ready to work, ready to learn. Problem is, who am

I to teach him? I haven't been here a year. Most of the medics
here have forgotten more than I've learned. In a vague sense,
I'm scared. Scared he'll fuck up, scared I'll fuck up. Scared for
our patients, for our jobs. I could bring this up, but there's no
point. Because people don't stop getting hurt just because the
medics on the other end of the phone aren't ready. The calls will
come in and we'll have to run them. More than that, I don't
say anything because though Marty claims he doesn't know
anything—and he truly doesn't—that fact doesn't bother him.
I don't know where it comes from, but he's bubbling over with
confidence. He's young and naive and totally devoid of body
hair, and yet here—saddled with a tough job he admits he's not
ready for—he's more relaxed than I am. He swigs from a Coke
bottle, blue Grady hat on backward.

"I'll figure it out," he says, "but in the meantime? Let me
know if I do anything stupid."

The dispatcher is chattering away in our ear, but we're no longer
listening. Once she gave us the complaint—person down, not
breathing, possible overdose—we tuned her out. There's nothing left to say. I'm driving, so Marty's the one who'll treat the
patient, the one who'll write the paperwork. Ultimately, the one
responsible. There's a rhythm to working an overdose, a sort of
easy glide that's nothing like the usual stomp and shuffle of a patient found not breathing. With an overdose, the situation is bad
but doesn't have to end badly. The trick is in understanding that
though the patient isn't breathing and may be a step away from
dead, if we get there fast and do everything right, if we keep
calm and don't panic—and *so many* people panic—we can save

him. Marty doesn't know any of this because he doesn't know anything. Sure, he's heard of the drugs people OD on, but he doesn't know what sort of evidence they leave behind. He doesn't know what to look for or where to find it, and when he can't, he doesn't know how to tease the details from nervous bystanders. He doesn't know which of the six things that all need to happen *right fucking now* he should do first. He just doesn't know how to run an overdose. And yet from the moment we arrive, he's a natural, a soothsayer, as if he's stepped outside of himself and is the only person capable of running this call.

It starts right away, as we're walking across the lawn. There's a guy standing at the door, big and doughy like Vince Vaughn in *Wedding Crashers*. He's frantic and trying to block our way. He's telling us that even though he's the one who called 911, he doesn't know anything, can't tell us anything. He wasn't here when it happened. And the patient? The one lying inside on the floor? They hardly know each other. Marty ignores him, doesn't say a word, simply pushes past the guy and goes in first, drug bag slung over his shoulder, arms slack at his sides.

The guy yells at Marty to stop and listen, to acknowledge that we understand that whatever happened here is—from a legal standpoint—not his fault. Marty keeps going, disappears into the house, a one-man armada navigating by instinct. The guy at the door is thrown off, his whole defense shot to hell because nobody's listening, nobody's hearing. The guy looks at me, desperate, as Marty aimlessly wanders the house, Moses trekking quietly across the linoleum. Finally, from somewhere inside, Marty's voice: "This him?"

The guy, flustered, follows. "Well . . . shit. Hold on."

I follow the guy into the house. We reach the bathroom and

there, on the tile floor, is our patient. There's a pulse, but he's not breathing.

"I don't know what happened," the guy says.

I suggest perhaps he fell from the sky. The guy looks at me, incredulous, and says, "You don't think it was an overdose?"

"Could be."

An overdose is almost mystical. It hinges on the slightest variation in dose or concentration or bad luck or something so inexplicable that we peg it to a full moon. It's one of Donald Rumsfeld's known unknowns. But there are hints. The trick is figuring out what the patient has taken based on what's lying around, since bystanders, friends, and family, however concerned they are, aren't going to rat out their friends.

Among the most popular drugs in Atlanta for plunging to the bottom of an ugly rabbit hole is GHB. It is, inconceivably, both a party drug and a date-rape drug. What got you high today may leave you unconscious tomorrow. Except more than unconscious—dead and unwakeable, a zombie in the depths of Haitian voodoo. On an ambulance, GHB appears in the form of a lifeless stripper we drag from the floor of a men's room, or a twenty-year-old we find facedown behind a midtown bathhouse. GHB is ingested and leaves no trace. We never know it's GHB but guess because the story fits. This story—a guy in his own house at five in the afternoon—doesn't fit.

That leaves opiates. They come in prescription form, but heroin is a whole lot cheaper, so that's usually what we see. Heroin is sold in black neighborhoods, but for whatever reason, it's consumed mostly by whites—cooks and waiters, generally, but also the occasional bored high school kid. What heroin does is calm the central nervous system. It says everything's okay, just slow down and don't worry. About anything. Not even that nagging voice somewhere deep inside that says it's been a while since I took a breath and maybe I ought to go ahead and take another. Just enough heroin is being kissed by God. Too much is a gentle ride to a breathless sleep.

This is what has happened to our patient, and upon seeing him, his friend has gotten dizzy. I push past, and he slumps against the doorway as we do our initial assessment. A quick scan of the room reveals a patient—painted asphyxiation blue— and a canvas shaving kit someone has tried to kick behind the toilet. I go for the shaving kit as Marty kneels over the patient, who's flat on his back, arms draped over his face—a giant despondent Smurf. I peek in the bag. Marty opens the airway. The bag is full of needles and heroin's powdery shadow; the airway is full of fluid.

When Marty asks if our patient does drugs, the friend, shocked and terrified, just stares. Marty flips on the suction unit and asks again, louder. The friend feels a police report coming and shakes his head, backing up, eyes locked on the vomit and spit swirling around the clear suction tubing. It's right here that most EMS crews begin ignoring the bystander or maybe get mad at him and start yelling. Marty shrugs. "Okay," he says, voice casual as if he might fall asleep midsentence. "Well, your buddy here? He's dead."

The friend goes pale and sweaty.

"I could probably do something," Marty says, "maybe even save him, if I knew what happened."

The friend's getting antsy because we're not doing anything, just waiting, so he asks if being high, is, well, if it's illegal. Marty grabs our ventilator and connects it to the oxygen as I reach into the drug bag and grab the Narcan. Marty tells him it's not illegal to be under the influence, just in possession. The friend turns to me, because I'm holding the canvas bag.

"If he stays dead," Marty says as he puffs a much needed breath of air into our patient's lungs, "the police will come. But if we know what's wrong and we treat him? Then we go to the hospital and the cops are none the wiser. You feel me?"

The friend feels him and it all comes gushing out. Everything we need to know plus a bunch more we really don't. We get to work in earnest but keep listening, because how addicted our patient is affects what happens next. What we need to know now is whether he's a casual user, once or twice a week, or does he do this every day? Because the guy who does this every day may well go into withdrawal and start seizing—from which he could die—if we totally remove the drug from his system. Which is what the Narcan does. So we need to know. Do I give him a lot and wake his ass up right now, or do I give him a taste, enough so he starts breathing but not enough for the brain to freak the fuck out? It's delicate, this part. Most people rush in and slam the Narcan, seizures be damned. Not Marty. He just waits.

"Once or twice a month," the friend says. "Maybe less."

Marty nods and thanks him, and I plunge a big thick needle into the rubber top of the Narcan vial and draw out two milliliters.

While I draw up the meds, Marty keeps ventilating. Though it would be easier and more effective to intubate him, we don't. The problem is, once we give him Narcan, he'll wake up. Narcan is a wonder drug, instantly and completely reversing the he's-not-breathing effect of narcotics. We've all heard stories of brand-new medics who've intubated patients and then given

Narcan. BOOM! The motherfucker jumps up, eyes wild, heart pounding, and takes off—with the ET tube crammed down his throat. What it must feel like to chase down a guy with an ET tube sticking out of his mouth—fearing that he'll outrun you, you'll lose him, and you'll have to explain it for the rest of your life—I can't begin to imagine.

Next I start an IV. Marty is proving himself a genius with the overdose, but I know damn well he can't start an IV. I drop to my knees, find a vein that hasn't been ruined by heroin, and slip the needle into our patient's yellow skin. Once I confirm the IV is good and tape it down, Marty tosses the BVM and grabs the patient's wrists. He winks at the friend. "Go ahead and back up, because it's about to get real in this little bathroom."

I depress the plunger, and two milliliters of Narcan disappear. In a few seconds there will be no heroin, just a sweaty patient, confused and ready to vomit. Marty starts the countdown as we wait for the freak-out.

One Mississippi, two Miss—

"WHOAWHATTHEFUUUUUUUCK!!!"

Marty smiles. One more white boy saved from oblivion.

26

Hearing Voices

Marty and I keep running calls, and each time I wait for the genius to shine through again, but it never does. Inexplicably, he has mastered nothing but the OD. The rest of the time, he's new and clueless. As for me, I don't have a specialty. At least not a medical one. What I have is a belief. It's probably misguided and definitely flies in the face of logic, not to mention the (usually) overwhelming evidence, but it's there all the same. I believe I can talk my way out of anything, diffuse any situation, talk anyone off any ledge. I always believe my patient—the one who's angry and violent, who's tearing up his mother's apartment—won't attack me. I may believe this, but Marty's skeptical, so I'm alone in the ambulance with Cordell.

Half an hour ago we got called out to a psych patient, possibly violent. We drove to the Greyhound station—a plate-glass eyesore oozing vagrants, addicts, and the occasional lost traveler into Atlanta's already beleaguered downtown—and realized we weren't here for just *any* violent psych patient.

"Tell me that's not Cordell," Marty said as we pulled up.

"Maybe he's calm tonight."

Cordell is a schizophrenic, a regular. He's chronically non-compliant with his meds, and when he goes off his meds, his mind catches fire. Even with our windows closed, we could hear him screaming.

Marty nodded. "Doesn't sound calm."

"No," I said. "He doesn't."

Marty wasn't in the mood for games. He wanted to call the cops and the fire department, wait for help to arrive, and then, with numbers, take Cordell down. Marty thought it'd be easier if we tied him to our stretcher and drowned him in a river of sedatives so he'd be snoring by the time we reached Grady. And we'd be well within our rights to do so. Cordell was screaming at passing cars and parked buses, at bystanders, the night sky, everything, at nothing. He'd attracted a crowd and was lashing out. Eventually, he'd hurt someone, maybe himself. Still, I thought we could handle this ourselves.

Cordell heard my door shut and turned. I was one of a dozen people standing around, but this uniform, this ambulance, they imply authority. Cordell stopped yelling. I'm not terribly big. Cordell is big. Three hundred pounds, six and a half feet tall, with bull shoulders that block out the light. Dressed in a windbreaker and dirty khakis, feet stuffed into size-fourteen sneakers with the heels crushed down so they're not sneakers anymore but slippers. A wild beard and an Afro bristling with lint and dead grass. He stomped over, angry and massive, a rhino escaped from the zoo.

He threatened us, threatened everyone. Told us to do whatever it was we came to do, because he wasn't cooperating. Marty, growing anxious, was ready to pull the trigger. But these calls require patience, and I'm nothing if not patient. I'm the steady drip that bores through stone. Calm down. Cooperate. Come with us. Or else.

Drip. Drip. Drip.

Cordell turned and charged us again. When he stopped a few feet away, we were in his shadow. He leaned forward, and Marty rocked back on his heels. Cordell blinked, and the sharp focus in his eyes softened to a dreamy haze. "Let me get my things."

So now we're in the ambulance, me writing a report, Cordell surrounded by a half-dozen overstuffed grocery bags. It's hard to say what calmed him down. I've come to think that all but the most unstable people know something's not right and, however reluctant, want to be helped. Sometimes I'm wrong. Last month we handled a woman whose body was right here in the Bluff but whose mind was in outer space. A cop had picked her up for walking in the street, and I climbed in the back of the cruiser next to her. Without warning, she pulled out a ten-inch butcher knife and tried to stab me. We were hip to hip in the backseat, her slashing wildly with the knife, me wiggling and scooting and trying not to get disemboweled.

Still. Cordell needs help, and tonight he agrees. There's only one place we can go. Thirteen.

Any patient who says he's crazy or that he wants to hurt himself or hurt somebody else or who talks about the government jamming microphones under his skin, he goes to Thirteen. The psych floor. Some buildings don't have a thirteenth floor, but here, in Atlanta, at Grady—one of the South's largest public hospitals—Thirteen's where they house the insane. Thirteen: two magical syllables spat out in contempt or spoken with reverence or whispered in fear. *Thirteen.*

Cordell says he's hearing voices. "I can't listen to them anymore," he says.

"What are they saying?"

He looks away, nodding and bobbing his shoulders, and the ambulance rocks like a small boat. He hears what I'm saying, but he can't focus—he's carrying on two conversations now.

You're worthless and stupid. Just a piece of shit. Your mama hates you, everyone hates you. So why are you still here? Why are you still talking? Why are you still alive?

"Have you been taking your medicine?"

Why haven't you killed that cracker-ass medic? Seriously. Nobody would care. Do it. Just do it. Right now. And when you're done, when he's dead, open the back door. Leap out of the ambulance. Splatter yourself all over the highway.

"Cordell . . ."

Do it.

Now.

He blinks and returns to the ambulance.

"What are they saying, Cordell?"

"Bad things. Mean things."

"Are they telling you to hurt yourself?"

He nods, and the ambulance crests another wave.

"They telling you to hurt other people?"

He shrugs. Looks away.

If he doesn't want to talk specifics, fine. There's nothing between us but a seat belt. No sense poking the bear.

"Can I ask you this, though?" I glance at the clock. "I'm guessing this didn't start now. It's probably been going on a while. So, it's what? Eleven-thirty? What changed to get you so worked up?"

"I'm rotting inside. I have to be ripped open so the foul can come out. I have to be relieved of this burden. To purge."

There's not a whole lot you can say to that.

"But they want me to wait."

"The voices?"

Another nod. "They said wait until midnight."

It's now 11:28. I shift in my seat. "You know, I'm guessing the doctors aren't gonna want that to happen." I shrug. "I don't want that to happen."

"If you tried to stop me, I'd have to kill you."

The next fifteen seconds pass in silence. Cordell doesn't sense my unease. That I've picked him up four or five times, that we've talked and joked and extended to each other a certain degree of mutual respect, doesn't, in his mind, preclude sudden senseless violence.

Up front, Marty stops at a red light.

It's 11:29. We have thirty-one minutes.

While we wait, Cordell crosses his legs so the untied size fourteen on his left foot dangles in midair.

"You got a little gum on your shoe, Cordell."

He shakes his head. It's not gum. It's a plug. "They're putting gasoline in my body. Every night. It goes in through that hole."

"Who is *they*?"

"Remove the gum and you can see all the way to my brain." He lets his foot drop back to the floor.

Eleven-thirty-three. Twenty-seven minutes and counting.

We're a few blocks out from Grady when my phone rings. Cordell strains against the seat belt. "Who's that? I said no one back here but us!"

Cordell reaches for his seat belt, and my stomach plunges. I yank out the phone. "Look! It's my phone. Just a phone. It's just us."

He stares at my phone while I tighten my grip on the heavy

laptop in my hands. If he attacks me, I'll raise this computer and bash in his head.

Cordell nods and settles back into his seat.

It's a relief when Marty finally pulls up to the ambulance ramp at Grady. I stand, lean over Cordell, and unbuckle his seat belt. He smiles, then grabs his bags and squeezes through the side door. We walk in, pass through triage, and head for the elevators. I move at a brisk pace. Cordell lumbers along behind me. He's got a slight limp and veers almost imperceptibly to the right, a battleship with an engine out. When we hit the elevators, it's 11:42. Eighteen minutes.

Grady is always crowded, and everyone wants to go up, down, anywhere but where they are, so no elevator is ever empty. Random people pile on, and eleven of the thirteen buttons between here and our final destination are pressed. After a prolonged interval during which I'm distracted by Cordell's hulking mass, we arrive at Thirteen.

Fifteen minutes to spare.

Outside the elevators, we're met by a security guard who sits alone at a table. One at a time, patients walk up and dump the contents of their mobile lives onto her desk. She sorts through crumpled bus maps, loose cigarettes, lighters, butter knives, old lottery tickets, broken sunglasses, and dirty underwear. Anything sharp, anything that can be broken and become sharp, anything someone can strangle himself with, anything that can be swallowed, it all gets confiscated.

The patients fuss and grumble, accuse her of stealing their stuff. *Last time I lost my paper clips. Last time you smoked my cigarettes. Last time that fat bitch stole my bra.*

Next to the table is a metal detector, and beyond that are the double doors leading to the psych wing. There's a man on the other side, visible only as a lone finger tapping on the glass. He's asking to be let out so he can smoke a cigarette. Just one. Real quick. After that he'll come right back. He promises.

I ask Cordell how he's doing, but there's no response. He rocks back and forth, both hands gripping his belly, fingers digging into the skin.

"Okay. Well, you just be cool and they'll get to us soon."

The next six minutes pass in a frustrating, clock-watching blur.

The guard is still checking bags. "Take everything out," she says over and over. "Your pockets, too. I have to see everything."

All the while, the man on the other side of the door keeps tapping on the glass, keeps asking to go out for a smoke, real quick, because after that he'll be right back. He promises.

"Next!"

I watch with vague interest as Cordell empties his pockets and the contents of his bags are cataloged. At last we're through and it's on to psychiatric triage.

Eleven-fifty. Ten minutes to go.

The staff tries to keep this area as calm as possible, but there's only so much they can do. It smells like dirty socks and is packed with people who, for one reason or another, need immediate psychiatric help. In the middle of the room is a glass-walled nurse's station, transparent and unhidden, so if a patient attacks the nurse, someone will see it right away. Tonight, naturally, it's empty. Where the nurse has gone or when she'll return, I have no idea. Cordell is starting to pace again. I tell him to relax, that we have all the time in the world. He just shakes his head. It's getting close to midnight and he knows it.

Cordell tries to sit, but the seats are taken. He backs against the wall, arms folded over his stomach. He's anxious, and the crowd in here isn't helping.

There's a woman wrapped in blankets spread out across three chairs, a man covered in grass and mud whom no one wants to sit next to, a furious-looking teenager talking to himself, and a couple—completely cracked out—pretending they don't need to be here. A lone man paces the room. His Members Only jacket is zipped up all the way, and his hat has CIA printed across the front in big yellow letters. He eases up next to me and leans in close. "I've lost my documents," he whispers. "All of them. My mints are gone, too."

It's 11:55 now, and Cordell throws a shoulder into the wall, shakes his head at some ethereal accusation, and stares at me with red, wild eyes. "I can't take this anymore," he stammers as sweat runs down his face. "I gotta do something."

"Just . . . just be cool. I'll get the nurse. Stay here."

I throw open the doors leading to an area marked STAFF ONLY and bang on the first door I come to. A slow-moving sleepy-eyed woman answers. "Look," I tell her, "you have a patient in triage who's threatening to kill himself. I need to speak to the nurse."

If she senses my urgency, it doesn't register on her face. She tells me flatly that the nurse will be with us in a moment. I look down at my watch. Thirty seconds. Maybe Marty was right. Maybe I should've sedated Cordell. I run back to triage, but when I get there, Cordell is nowhere to be found. The CIA man is still there, though.

"You haven't seen my mints, have you?"

I spin around, looking for a place a three-hundred-pound

man could hide. And there it is: the bathroom. I rush over and grab the handle, but the door's locked.

Three, two, one. Midnight.

And then a calm voice from beyond the door. "Who's there?"

"Cordell? What are you doing?"

"Relieving myself."

"You're what?" I ask.

"I'm relieving myself."

I laugh. My back is covered with nervous sweat, and I lean my head against the wood.

"I haven't had a good movement in a week," he says. "The gasoline, it binds me up. And this is the only place they can't infiltrate."

"So that's what you meant by . . . Good. Good. That's really good news, Cordell."

"Can I have some privacy?"

"Sure."

I don't know what happened to Cordell after we left. I don't know what treatment he underwent, how long it took to silence the voices, how long he remained on Thirteen. It's hard to keep track of any patient, let alone one locked behind the padded walls of Grady's psych ward. I do know we saw him again, but everything that preceded our next meeting had been lost amid the shifting sands of his chemically imbalanced mind. It's not so for everyone. Some people love to talk, need to talk. Deacon Brown is one of those people. He's been on Thirteen, and he'll share his story with anyone who'll listen.

"My name's Deacon Brown. I was abducted by aliens."

Right now he's got a man by the arm and is telling his story. "I'm not kidding," he says. "Aliens. Snatched me right up." Deacon's the first to admit he's an alcoholic. He's also, unapologetically, a repeat offender. "I'm a mess," he says, staring into the man's face with those big yellow eyes. "Look at me. Sheeit, I'm wearin' someone else's pants." None of that matters. He's crazy and he's got problems, maybe, but that doesn't make him a liar. "Aliens," he says. "Honest to Christ."

His abduction happened on Ponce. He was sleeping off a bender in a little patch of weeds next to the grocery store when, out of nowhere, a flash of light. Blinding. Whole damn world lit up. And then, before he knew it, hands. A whole mess of them. Reaching out from the big nothing, grabbing him, lifting him. He didn't go easy. Aliens or not, you weren't just gonna snatch Deacon Brown from a good sleep. He kicked, he yelled, he threw a few punches, but what can one man do? Against aliens. Nobody goes through the trouble of flying in from another galaxy to be fought off by a single drunk. So up he went. Levitation.

And then he was aboard the ship. Nothing but blaring lights and cold steel. The aliens held his arms and his legs, took his clothes, even took away his box cutter. Then they tied him down. Above he saw a glimmer: something long and sharp and probably lethal coming right at him. He screamed. His skin was pierced and he felt a burning sensation, as if being cooked from the inside. The last thing he remembered was a terrible salty taste in his mouth, as if the whole ocean had washed over him. And then he passed out.

The noise woke him. Then there was the motion, constant

and jarring. How long he'd been out, where he was, he couldn't say. He knew only that he was alive, and whether that was a good thing, he also couldn't say. He opened his eyes in time to see his left arm pinched off and once again everything going black. They weren't done with him. More arrived, too many to count—lines of them, waves, like Chinese soldiers cresting a hill. Each time he looked up, more had been let loose upon him. His skin was pierced again and again. Even his dick, man, they put something up his dick, and whatever you wanna say about creatures that travel halfway across the universe just to fuck with a dude, you enter a whole new realm when you touch a man's dick.

Days later, months later, maybe a year later, he woke up here. At Grady. He's lost weight, he thinks. He knows for sure he's a good two inches shorter. Whatever it was they did to his left arm, it's back on, stronger than ever. They cured him of the booze, too, but he'd kill for a cigarette.

"That's it," he says. "Start to finish. Aliens snatched me up, and I don't know where they took me, but I'm here now." Deacon leans back, spreads his arms. "I don't know a motherfucking thing. Except I'm broke. So, you got a dollar? Maybe two?"

Marty and I are just showing up at work. And though we don't hear the story, we see the hand extended, the awkward smile of the man Deacon has cornered. The guy has wide, terrified eyes. He's a tourist, maybe, or the uncle of a patient, and he's just in town to deliver flowers or dinner, and then he's off, back in his car to leave Atlanta and all its madness behind.

We *could* tell him. We could explain this is just Deacon, that he drinks but never takes his medicine and sometimes he has to be picked up and brought in. We could say that we brought

Deacon here two days ago. We could point out that the story he's telling now, about the aliens and the probes, the bright lights, that was us. But we don't.

Instead, we walk a wide arc. We keep going and the man stays where he is, simultaneously transfixed and terrified. This story, this moment, will live on forever. He'll tell his grandkids this story. And it'll all be true.

"I was abducted by aliens," Deacon says. "Snatched me right up. Honest to Christ."

27

Nobody Dies Tonight

Marty doesn't think anybody's dead. He's shaking his head at the dispatcher, as if she's not just a voice but right here with us. "This is bullshit," he says as he flips on the sirens. We're on our way to Pine Street, the city's largest homeless shelter, for a man who's down and possibly dead. Or not. "I'm deader than this motherfucker is," Marty says, shaking his head again. "I can promise you that."

"Can you stop saying that?" I'm treating patients tonight and Marty's driving, which means if this guy is really dead, I'll be the one to deal with it. "You're gonna jinx us."

He's undeterred. "These guys call all the time," he says. "And it's always bullshit. Dude's not dead."

"Feel good enough to bet on that?"

"That he's not dead?"

"That he's not dead."

He smiles as he blows through an intersection, sirens screaming. "Okay. Yeah." He's nodding. Confident. "If he's dead, I'll run the whole call."

"Paperwork, too," I add.

"Fine."

We shake. "But you're gonna lose," Marty says. "Because this dude's not dead."

He's probably right. We bet all day—that someone's not dead or that the psych patient in the library won't be wearing pants—and from experience, I can say that I've likely made a bad bet. When someone calls 911, a dispatcher answers and asks a series of leading questions to determine the nature of the emergency. Most people will, when asked, say the symptoms are worse than they are. So bleeding is always heavy, pain is always severe, and birth is always imminent, even when it's not. Sometimes it's because callers are hysterical and overreact, but often it's because if they say it's anything other than a full-on emergency it'll take an ambulance twenty minutes longer to arrive. If they say he's dying, it'll only take six.

Marty whips the ambulance up to the shelter and groans. It's massive and in the middle of the city, long ago condemned but, inexplicably, still open. It specializes in loitering. During the day, hundreds of men crowd the surrounding blocks, arguing, fighting, pissing, getting high, getting arrested. It's worse at night. Those who fail to get a bed, those who got a bed but now want out because their skin is crawling and they need more, those who never wanted a bed, just another hit, they're all wandering the streets. They crowd the vacant lots, pour from the surrounding crack motels, and creep through the shadows of Renaissance Park.

There are only two entrances to the shelter. Marty grabs the radio and asks the dispatcher which side our patient is on. She isn't sure and tells us to stand by. We're hoping to hear he's by the main entrance. The main entrance leads to the upstairs, where there are fewer people. The upstairs is also home to a strange vortex—a large open room divided into plywood cubicles serving as permanent residences for a lucky few. There are truths in this universe so confounding, they were never meant to be revealed. How a man becomes a permanent resident of a homeless shelter—is he still homeless?—is one of them. So I don't ask. But the front door is in and out; it's quick and painless and as easy as a call here can get. The side door is something different altogether.

The dispatcher comes over the air. "Use the side entrance," she says. "Someone's waiting for you there."

Shit.

We weave down the steep slope of the side street—taking care not to run over any of the jaywalkers—then step out of the ambulance and onto the stained pavement. We're immediately assaulted by a wave of sounds and smells, a flowing river of humans living but just barely. Here the double doors are swung wide, but it's so dark, we can't see beyond the airless threshold. A man in a black shirt that says ENFORCEMENT leans against the wall smoking. He is probably our guide, but it's hard to say. He ignores us—uniforms, ambulance, all of it—until we enter his personal space and confirm that we've arrived because someone called 911. He nods and finishes his cigarette, then crushes it out. "Yeah, all right," he says. "Y'all follow me."

A few seconds later, we're in the dayroom. Hundreds of men sleeping in chairs, playing cards, talking to themselves. Some spend their days arguing, others—feverish sentries—stand guard over their bags. The careless few will have their prescription drugs stolen by the sharks who prey on the weak. The lighting is dim, and everything's made of crumbling concrete. The air is heavy with stink and activity. We can hardly see to pick our way through.

Every few feet someone yells, "Here go your patient!" to the delight of his friends. Others shuffle up alongside us, ghosts in the musty air, and ask about boils, cuts, abscessed teeth, gangrenous fingers. We push on into the dark, past the yelling, laughing, cussing, and horrible tubercular coughing. Past the makeshift altar where a chubby preacher shouts over the noise: "And you must say unto Him, Lord Jesus, I give myself over to You, for Thou art King!"

We do a quick sweep of the dayroom, the bunk room, and the showers. Enforcement has a radio in his hand, and he's talking into it, but whoever's on the other end has no better idea where our patient is than he does. Finally, he stops and says, "Guess he's in the basement, then."

Lucky us.

And so we descend, step by step, into the black nothing. We weave through halls stinking of mold and filthy bodies, boots sticking to the floor with each step, telling ourselves, as if we need reminding, that this is *not* how we wanted to start the day. On the stairwell, weighed down with forty or fifty pounds of equipment, we pass a ghost—bone-thin and wearing ragged clothes—who shakes his head and says, "Motherfucker don't look good at all." Anticipation is usually the most dramatic part of a call, but sometimes when we get there—especially when our escape route is this treacherous, the onlookers this curious— the moment lives up to its billing. Like today. Our patient is sprawled on the basement floor, violently convulsing. He's surrounded by a crowd of gawkers and medical theorizers: *I seen that shit before. That shit right there AIDS.*

Marty nudges me. "Told you he wasn't dead."

The bystanders remain by our side. Half-drugged and quite possibly insane, they're down here for any number of reasons.

Boredom and curiosity, for starters. There's also a lunatic fringe convinced they can help, as well as a strange minority pushed to the edge of tears for a man they don't know.

We don't put down our gear because, as with our shoes, it'll stick to the floor. Instead, we treat our patient holding the weight of everything we own, like Atlas. I grab a needle, clench it between my teeth like a pirate, reach into the drug bag, grab our anti-seizure meds, and plunge the needle into the vial. I push in one CC of air, then watch the bubbles ride to the top and draw out a CC of seizure-stopping benzodiazepine. Next I purge the air from the syringe, flick the excess off the needle, and jab it into the patient's leg. I depress the plunger and wait. It's not working. The patient keeps on seizing. The onlookers, with all their medical knowledge, get antsy. They want results, they want a cure. They haven't started making demands and taking action, but they will if— Wait. His convulsions stop. A calm settles over the men in the filthy basement. Then, in reverent tones, a voice: "Damn. That right there is some heavy shit. Heavy fucking shit."

Right about now is when people make assumptions. Like the assumption that this guy, gurgling and seizing in the basement of a homeless shelter, probably doesn't take his medicine. Or that even if he does, he probably drinks heavily, which negates the effects of his meds. Either way, it's safe to assume that he's another bum letting his life slip through his fingers. But too often assumptions are wrong. While I'm checking vitals, Marty does a quick sweep for injuries. Is he bleeding or broken or injured in some way that suggests he didn't come down here and seize but maybe fell or was thrown down the stairs? Marty is looking for something, anything, to prove that what's going on perhaps isn't as it appears. He runs his hand beneath the man's head and comes up with a bloody glove. We roll him and Marty finds the laceration—a big fat set of pursed lips on the back of his head. Marty presses on them, and the hard skull beneath gives way. It's been fractured, which means his brain is bleeding, and that's probably why he was seizing and will probably start seizing again. Why he might still die. Time to hurry.

We need help carrying him out, but we're in the basement of a large brick building. No radio reception. No one to call. We're on our own. For five minutes we struggle to get the man immobilized, to suction out his mouth, to get him on oxygen, and painfully, to get him up the stairs. Halfway up, he starts seizing again and needs more medicine.

Upstairs we have light, but things don't get any easier. The crowd closes in. They push and yell, some trying to clear a path, others intentionally stopping progress. They scream at each other, at us. Some ignore the man and ask what we can do for a stomachache. The preacher fights his way through the crowd, steps in front of us, and lays a hand on the man's chest. The patient begins to convulse again. "This man needs prayer," the preacher says.

I've had enough, and I ram the stretcher into the preacher's gut. "I already prayed," I tell him, "and God told me to get his ass to the hospital."

With that, we're gone.

28

Another Day in Paradise

People who know us, who've heard these stories and laughed with us and at us—people who've worried over us—wonder what our days look like. They try to imagine the two of us charging through Atlanta, seeking out the best of the worst. "It's how we've always told it," I say. "It's exactly the way you think it is."

Even when you work nights, every day is the same. An ambulance is a conveyor belt, emergency medicine a factory. Hearts, kidneys, lungs, legs—the raw materials of a functioning human—pass down the assembly line. Each is broken and will be fixed. Quickly, though. More are coming. The gears turn, the furnace glows. Smoke puffs into the air.

Salvation through repetition. This I can do because I have done it before—it's half prayer, half truth, a whisper in a hurricane of self-doubt. If the possibility of saving a life comes down to routine, to muscle memory, then every shift must begin the same way. I pack a lunch, shower, and slip into my uniform. Atlanta is beyond hot, it's jungle-humid. Rain is always falling or threatening to fall or maybe just fell, so the leaves hang fat from the trees and clouds of steam rise up from the streets. The starched collar, the heavy pants, the black boots—I'll sweat all night.

As I hop in the car and leave the neighborhood, I wave to people coming home from work. It's always then, as I'm leaving, that my mind wanders off to the same ghost story. What would happen if someone came to the door, our door? Would the explosion of barking dogs scare them away, would the lock hold, and what about the door itself? Did my wife remember to charge her cell phone, and is it sitting next to her, close enough that she can grab it and call for help as someone kicks in the door, because no, the door won't hold. Not with someone kicking it. They never do. And this man, now that he's in my house, would he stay downstairs, would he steal the TV and the computer, the camera, and then disappear into the night, or would he go upstairs? Is the alarm set, and how fast will the police respond? What about the gun? It's up there, loaded and ready, a shock and awe in miniature that Sabrina and I are licensed to carry but not conceal. I feel better knowing it's there, but in the hysteria and panic that a home invasion surely must be, will Sabrina have the presence of mind to cock it and aim it—to shoot someone? What if she misses? Will there be time for another round, or will that be it? And if that's it, if things end badly, will I ever be able to work this job again? Or will I be too bitter, too angry, too suspicious that the perpetrator—certainly uncaught, because nobody gets caught—is sitting right there, across from me, wincing in pain as I splint his broken arm?

I think this every night, but only as I leave, and each time, as my car pulls out of the neighborhood, I swear I'll stop working nights. But I never do.

The drive is twenty minutes of peace. I listen to a Fresh Air podcast: Terry Gross's calming voice is worlds away from Grady. I'm somewhere else entirely until I arrive. I pull into the parking deck and walk past the hospital. Patients and family members mill around, and so do the homeless, looking for money or drugs, looking for a way to get back inside and off the street before the sun sets. Inside the EMS area, the day-shift crews sit around talking. One by one the night crews trickle in, and for a brief moment we mingle, night and day, joking and laughing, talking shit, taking shit. We night-shifters joke about their day because it's over, but they never joke about ours because it hasn't yet begun. That's just a rule, simple as that. You can say I suck and that I wouldn't have been able to handle your shit-kicker, but to say you hope I catch one, no. You'd never do that. Not more than once, anyway. After ten minutes of shit talk, the day-shifters go home and we go to work, and after everything that's been said, they still turn to us, look us in the eye, and say, "Be safe," and when they say it, they mean it. *Be safe.*

I clock in and start my prep ritual. I dump my gear by the back door of the ambulance and slip on a pair of gloves, grab a rag and a bottle of disinfectant, and remove all traces of the previous inhabitants. Nothing is spared: the seats, the cabinets, the parts of the stretcher that the patient touches, the parts that only I touch. I clean the door handles and the silver bar mounted on the ceiling that runs the length of the patient compartment, because everyone reaches up and steadies himself on it, taking hold with a bloody and infected hand.

Then I go through the equipment, one piece at a time, to see that it's there and ready to be used. More than that, really, because even if it's there, it needs to be there in the way I want it to be there. Everyone has his own way of running calls, of managing the unmanageable, a sort of personal arithmetic, and it's this style that dictates how I set up the ambulance. There are people who can't run a call without everything set up just so. I am not one of those people, but I'm close. Once the ambulance is clean, I slip a key into the ignition. The diesel engine rattles to life.

Once Marty arrives, he snaps a battery in the radio and keys up to go in-service. It's five in the afternoon, so the second we appear on the dispatcher's screen, we catch a call. Usually it's something close. Unless the bottom has dropped out and there are no ambulances anywhere—which is to say there are ambulances everywhere—and then we will be sent off to some far corner of the city. Sometimes it's for a toothache that dispatch couldn't hold on to anymore. Sometimes it's a real-life dead person who's been waiting and waiting, and now it takes us twenty minutes to get there.

But not today. Today when we go in-service, there are four available ambulances out of a possible twenty-five, so the call we catch is downtown. It's an alcoholic who made it all the way to the door of the liquor store, shaking and trembling, before his disease said "Fuck it," and now he's in full-blown withdrawal and seizing on the sidewalk. A fish plucked from the water, left flopping on the ground. It's just a short drive, barely around the corner, so we won't have much time to shake off the rust and slip back into the subtle but constant vigilance born of waiting for the Big One.

When we get out, the sun is blazing. My feet melt inside my big black boots. We give the alcoholic Valium, but he keeps on seizing, never stops seizing. We drop him off at the hospital and nothing has changed, except the nurse has asked Marty out, so at least there's that.

Before we even clear Grady, our radio is chirping. Dispatch has something for us. "It's right out front," she says. "In the bus stop."

We ask what's going on, but she's dodgy and uncertain. All she knows is that the scene is safe. "Just drive around front and have a look."

We find him at a bus stop, waiting. Not for us, but waiting. Waiting to die or for all this to pass. Maybe he's just waiting for his bus, it's hard to say; he isn't much for conversation. I stop about two feet from him and lean against the wall. Marty stays a good ten feet behind me, close enough to know he doesn't want to get any closer. It's hard to blame him. The guy is sitting with his legs crossed, casual as can be, while maggots eat his face.

They've made off with nearly the entire left side, from his nose all the way to his ear, and from his eyebrow down to his jawline. All that skin, all that rotten and rotting flesh, is being consumed—while we watch, while he sits quietly on the bench. There are hundreds of maggots, all jockeying for position, and every few seconds a maggot slips off the cliff edge of his face and tumbles through the air and onto the pavement below. I've never seen anything like it.

From the safety of his observation post, Marty asks what's going on. The man reaches up and presses the back of his left hand into his eye, forcing out a stream of blood and furious white larvae. "Skin cancer," he says as he wipes his hand on his shirt. He has melanoma and it got infected, but he's tired of the doctors and the nurses and the tests, all of it, and decided to leave. So he walked out and spent the night in the bushes across the street from Grady, where a swarm of flies landed and planted all the babies that have made such short work of his face. Another squeeze of the eye, another trickle of blood, more angry maggots. Marty backs up.

"You gotta get up," I say. "You have to come inside."

"Why?"

"Because you have maggots on your face. Because they're eating you, literally. As we speak, they're devouring you. I think your eye is gone, and who knows what's next, so come on, get up. Please."

He reaches up again with his left hand, and somewhere behind me, Marty threatens to pass out. The man is unmoved. He's done with hospitals and doctors and procedures. And though it might not be done with him, he's done with cancer. He recrosses his legs, rubs his eye. "I'm not going back in there," he says. "I don't want to, and I don't have to."

A bus pulls up. Passengers get on, passengers get off. Atlanta's quotidian life marches on.

We call a doctor. He brings a wheelchair, and from behind it he talks to this man who last night was his patient but now is being eaten by bugs. The doctor speaks in the sweet voice of final authority; he is the man who can, with a shrug, send our patient back to the bushes to be eaten alive. It works. The patient stands and plops down in the wheelchair. I grab the handles and push. Marty trails, careful not to step on any of the maggots, all of them tiny squiggling urns, fat with the remains of a man not yet dead.

That was an intense start to the day, but it's just the start. We've been here two hours. Once we clear Grady, we're sent to a post. We drive to a place where we can stare through the windshield and watch the world pass by. All the while, the radio chatters, it never stops chattering—the dispatch radio is like a thirteen-year-old girl at a sleepover. Tonight we're lucky; everyone else is getting the calls. Where that leaves us is coverage. The ambulance from Simpson Road catches a call, so we go to Simpson Road. The ambulance downtown catches a call, so we go downtown. We shuffle from post to post for a couple of hours, and slowly, almost accidentally, rush hour is over. The sun dips below the trees. The world recharges, prepares to repurpose itself. So we get a chance to eat dinner, listen to a Braves game. Marty screams at the radio. "Uggla? Again? Fucking Uggla."

It's ten o'clock and the party's over. The city is refilled and calls are picking up. We catch one and get sucked back into the machine—it'll be two or three before we break free.

They start out as medical calls, chest pain and abdominal pain, dizziness, nausea, seizures. Maybe it's a child with a roach in her ear, which we'll coax out with a flashlight and some saline. None of these are serious, and all of them go to Grady. One after another after another until the triage nurses are cursing and begging us not to come back. Around eleven-thirty the drunks start to call. Or rather, the people with the drunks start to call. People waiting to get into clubs who can't keep their mouth shut, so someone else shuts it for them. Drunks behind the wheel who drifted right, overcorrected, and rolled in the middle of the street. Rag dolls with ignition keys. They get out and are wandering, scared but unharmed, when we arrive. Some of the drunks will be pissed to see us; some won't even notice. A few of the women will be amorous, all sly smiles, fingernails brushing my thigh as they reach for my dick and smile. "Yeah, I'ma get me some of that."

We run these calls until one A.M. and then, in the unlikeliest of places, catch a break. Posted down in the Pittsburgh neighborhood where everyone carries a knife and we run more stabbings than shootings, we gratefully find ourselves not busy. We get out, lean on the hood of the ambulance, and talk. Hookers wander by. A few stop and talk, some out of boredom, but some ask for sheets or sterile water. Extra gloves. God only knows what they do with the gloves.

Homeless guys wander by, but it's too late to beg, too late for anything but drugs, and we don't have drugs. Packs of girls walk by, loud and laughing, slapping at their weaves because weaves itch, and there's no way to scratch, so they just slap. Once in a while a couple of guys in their twenties—known as Young Boys to everyone who lives here—walk by, and if they're trying to look tough, they'll scowl, but if they're for real, they'll just nod and keep walking. We've spent enough time in shark-infested waters to instinctively distinguish between a predator and his prey. A guy who's for real is slow-moving and self-assured, possessed of an almost casual disregard for everyone. Nothing left to prove, he simply is. People who live here see it, too, and they go silent as he walks by. Even birds stop chirping when the lion stirs.

Then, in the darkness, our number is called. The dispatcher's voice is rushed, and we know right away that our long dry spell of running nothing but nothing has come to an end. Something bad is headed our way.

Really, she's been there all along. Her entire life has been leading to this moment; hers is a very secular kind of predestination. Tonight she's finally stepped off the curb and into a dark street,

or popped that ballooning aneurism, or sat across from her husband as he cleaned his gun and wondered—while she peeked
down the long steel barrel—if he remembered to unload it.
Bang, and her moment has arrived.

Tonight it comes as a surprise for her but not for us. We
knew she was out there somewhere, and while we handed out
spare gloves to hookers, her countdown reached zero. Tick-tock-
tick. That bad call, the one we knew was out there, is no longer
merely waiting but coming for us, a bull let loose and charging,
the heavy pounding of hooves. Nothing but horns and muscle
and fury.

We're dispatched out to a wreck. A Caprice Classic that was
T-boned by an Escalade. The Caprice got hit so hard and skidded so far that two of the wheels were shorn off at the axle. Both
cars were full of people, and when we arrive, they're all out,
walking and confused, crying, yelling, bleeding. Some are hurt
and a few aren't. We pick our way through the crowd as more
ambulances show up. A fire engine blasts the night apart with
its horns. The front-seat passenger took the brunt of the hit,
and she's pinned beneath the caved-in door of the Caprice. Her
pelvis is broken; the femur is a memory. Her right lung has been
punctured, and all hell is breaking loose inside her skull. She has
seizure after seizure after seizure as the fire department tries to
cut her out.

None of the firemen is a medic, so one throws a coat over
my shoulders and lets me into the car—the hot zone is what
they call it—where I start an IV and pump her with round after
round of seizure-stopping benzodiazepines, which tonight don't
help. All this is taking forever, and the hospital has already called
back to see where the hell we are.

"Yeah, Doc, I know we've been here a while, but she's stuck."

"What do you mean, *stuck*?"

So we wait. The fire department cuts. The patient seizes. The Golden Hour—the sixty minutes between insult and surgery that we give a critical patient before her chances of survival drop—tick-tick-ticks away. I'm really sweating, brushing up against all this broken and slowly-being-cut-into metal. Marty stands on the fringe as his phone blows up. That nurse from earlier will . . . not . . . quit. "I know you're working tonight, but call me as soon as you're off. I'm drunk. And I have no idea where I left my underwear."

Finally, the saws break through and she's free.

As we're leaving, a cop asks me for a prognosis, but he already knows what I'm going to say; he's got a can of spray paint in his hand and he's shaking it, cap off, as he's asking the question. Before I've said, "Not good," he's turning and drawing white paint lines around everything in the road: tires and debris, shoes, purses, ejected car seats, and when they're in the road, ejected people. If she dies tonight, that cop will come back with an investigative team. They'll close off the road. They'll study the paint lines, re-create the scene. They'll determine fault.

Then we transport. The back of the ambulance is nothing but blood and glass, cut-off clothes, and a used ventilation bag. The suction tubing is full of blood, though almost none of it has made it down into the canister. At Grady, the doctor listens to my report as he checks the patient's abdomen for internal bleed-ing. I tell him about the cars, what kind they were, how they looked, how the other passengers looked. Where she was seated and whether she was entrapped. I tell him she never stopped seizing. She's rolled off the backboard, and someone lubes a gloved finger and slips it up her ass to check for rectal tone. The glove snaps as it's stripped off and the voice yells that the rectal tone is good, which negates a spinal injury, and that's better than nothing. Then she's wheeled off to surgery, and while she's still alive, whether or not she'll live is hard to say. Sometimes it's worse than it looks.

It's almost three. The hours between two and four go one of two ways: Either the city releases us from its grip and we scurry to a corner for fitful rest; or it doesn't. And this time of night, when it doesn't let us go, what it gives us is something strange.

I usually forget everything I do after three A.M. Amnesia brought on by exhaustion, by the impenetrable darkness of a road with no streetlights. There are entire calls, start to finish, that will never leave me. My three A.M. calls won't be among them. Recently, someone asked if I remembered running a white guy in an all-black neighborhood. "You remember," the guy said, "he was dead for so long, he was stuck to the carpet. Remember that?" I didn't remember. Not that he was stuck to the carpet, or that when the cops showed up, everybody in the house claimed not to know who this white stranger was or how long he'd been dead on the floor. I'd forgotten it all.

This morning we catch a call for a woman with back pain. We drive over, get out, and knock on the door. She yells for us to come in. We walk to the bedroom and find her lying naked in bed. She's got the sheets thrown back, goose bumps run over her arms, her bare legs, and across her stomach. Marty is shocked, scandalized, and embarrassed. He looks away, face red. "Uh . . ."

I'm behind him, holding our bag. I gently ease around him.

Smile. In my experience, the more you try to pretend you aren't staring, the more it looks like you're staring. We are, after all, professionals. Besides, if she's not embarrassed, why should I be? I'm not naked.

"What's going on?" I ask, casual, like this is any other call.

"I threw my back out masturbating," she says. "That's my dildo." She points to the nightstand. We look, and sure enough, her giant rubbery dildo winks at us from its perch. For a moment the only sound is the soft rumble of its vibration. It's three-thirty in the morning.

Now I'm embarrassed.

"Um . . ."

She smiles. "Is this common?"

"I don't think so," I say. "Then again, I don't use one. But I've never seen this, if that's what you mean." I clear my throat. "Would you like me to cover you up?"

"Why? Would it help? Ya know, the heat?"

"No."

"Then I'm fine." She curls her toes, and I stare at her feet, trying to ignore her breasts, trying to pretend I haven't noticed it's time for another Brazilian. "If I start nipping out, you'll know I'm cold."

I've seen hundreds of people too sick to care that they're naked. This woman is one of only two who has seemed to enjoy it.

"So we need to get you onto our stretcher. Can you slide over, or do we need to pick you up?"

She shakes her head. "I can't sit up at all. Whole back's locked up."

We crawl over to get her, and now it's the three of us in bed together—her naked, us in our purple rubber gloves. The mattress is soft and worn out, so it's almost a waterbed, and our weight creates a big cozy depression. We sink in. We slide down and there's no stopping it. It's like wrestling in outer space—we're slow and awkward and unable to stop ourselves from falling on the bed, on her, on each other. I'd laugh if this weren't so awkward, so outrageously inappropriate.

Finally, she's out of bed and onto our stretcher. She's covered with a sheet and buckled in. Marty grabs her robe, drops it on her lap. We turn off the lights but leave the vibrator on. It rumbles away as we walk out the door. *Mmmmmmmmm . . .*

Around four A.M. is when people wake up dead. A woman rolls over and notices her husband is cold and stiff, too silent to be anything but gone. Maybe Aunt Gladys got up in the middle of the night, and it's not until four-thirty that someone hears her gurgling in the bathroom. It's hard to run a call like that at this hour because we're exhausted, and the last thing we want is to slip-slide through two-hour-old urine to drag Aunt Gladys out of the bathroom in her wet robe while she strokes out.

Every blip of the radio makes my heart pound with fear. *Please, God, do not let us catch a bad call right now. It's almost time to go.*

Time unwinds slowly, as if the clock is not merely an object but a cruel and calculated tormentor—the indifferent hour hand, the sadistic minute hand . . . it's torture. The final forty minutes of the shift are waterboarding in fluid Swiss motion. We stare out the window. The sun's not up, but it's close—the hint of light is there, levity after a long black night. And then mercy. A dispatcher comes over the radio and sets us free.

We throw it in gear and race through the streets. We're tired and we're beaten, but we're going home.

By the time we hit the gas station, the sky is no longer black but gray, a thin line of silt blue visible in the east. With the windows cranked down and fresh air streaming in, the city isn't so mean. Back at Grady, we restock the equipment, wipe down the ambulance, and turn in our keys. We talk to the day crews and tell them what we did, how they *never* could have done it—not like us, no way in hell—until it's time for them to clock in and take over. They're day-shifters, so they're weak, they're backups—except they're family, too. *Be safe, guys. Be safe.*

Minutes later, I walk past the hospital, sneaking around the homeless guys waking up. Then I'm in my car and out on the streets and at last I can say the words: *It's quiet.* Back at home, I strip down and shower. Sabrina isn't awake, not yet. I slip between the sheets and know there's nothing to do but sleep. Real, genuine sleep. No ambulance, no radio, no one waiting to die.

I'm unconscious before the bed knows I'm here.

29

A Long Answer to a Stupid Question

The clerk is horrified. I'm standing before him in a bloodstained shirt, my eyes red from not sleeping. The blood is Gumby's, and it's smeared across my stomach as if somebody sponged it on. Marty and I ran a call this morning, tiny little Toyota versus dump truck that went exactly the way it should have. The Toyota was broadsided, and the driver's door was punched in thirty-six inches. The impact was so intense, the gas cap popped off. That cap—black molded plastic worn brittle by spilled gas—was the first thing I saw when we got on-scene. The next was Gumby. He was slouched over the console, a broken and pulpy mess, his body contorted into something less than human but, remarkably, alive. His face was purple and swollen. How old he was, I couldn't say. But he had a flattop shaved at a slant that looked like Gumby's head. So we called him Gumby.

Extrication took forever. Minutes, hours, days, I don't really remember. Almost without our noticing, he was cut free and in the back of our ambulance. We worked him all the way to the hospital—suction and oxygen and a pair of huge IVs—and I wasn't careful enough to make sure that big floppy hair didn't touch me. I didn't notice the blood on my shirt in the ambulance or at the hospital or even as I clocked out. Who looks at his own stomach? But now I'm here in the hardware store, trying to buy a new plunger, and the clerk has brought it to my attention. "I hope that's not real," he groans, pointing to my stomach.

"As long as it's not mine" is all I say in reply. I hold out my credit card, but he isn't ready to move on, is either unwilling or unable to complete our transaction.

The interrogation continues. "Did he live?"

"Last I knew."

"What happened?" Before I can answer: "I bet you see some horrible things."

"I guess you do, too. I mean, you've seen me."

But he's in no mood for jokes. "What's the worst thing you've ever seen?"

Again with this fucking question.

There's a line behind me, people who no doubt normally resent any delay not of their own making, though they, too, have forgotten their purchases and are leaning in to hear what I have to say. The patch on my shoulder says Grady, and the bloodstain on my shirt says, *Yes. The rumors you've heard, they're all true.* Except they're not. Grady's an incredible place, but it's just that—a place—and being a medic is a job, something I do to make money. Money I use to buy things. Like plungers. Except when I can't. Like right now.

He's waiting. Hoping all the tax dollars spent to train, equip, and pay me will pay off in the form of a story he can tell his friends later tonight. Who knows, maybe if it's good enough, he'll keep it around awhile, use it to drive home his point that dealing with the public is simultaneously enlightening, enthralling, and infuriating and that, as such, retail truly is the tip of the psychoanalytical spear. The people behind me are waiting for a good story, too, and why not. They're out buying plungers on a Tuesday morning. Anything is better than this.

The question doesn't offend me. Some of my coworkers, if you were to ask them this question, they'd hit you. Others would ignore you. Some would make a big show of explaining why such a question is not merely impolite but flat-out offensive. Me, I don't mind. Though, frankly, it is a strange thing to ask—I mean, do you really want to hear about the child born with fetal alcohol syndrome whose stepfather burned him every day with cigarettes? I wouldn't. There are some brutal motherfuckers out there, why can't we just leave it at that?

But we can't. People ask, and I guess it's because they've never had reason to contemplate the question, so it's not until they begin to hear the answer that they realize how strange a door they've opened. Some of them, before I get going, get squeamish and cut me off. Others lose interest and change the subject, asking me something else while I'm midsentence and in full swing. A small minority walk away, unimpressed. This final group has watched too much TV and they're expecting more—the half-cooked remains of a baby left in the microwave—and anything less is pedestrian. Sometimes they interrupt with their own horror story, followed always by "I bet you ain't never seen nothing like that." To which I say, "A motherfucker who's not only rude but full of shit? No, I've seen plenty of them."

So yeah, I answer the question. It's just that I do it my own way. This person, whom I don't even know, has entered uninvited into my world, so he'll get what I feel like giving him, which is never the worst thing I've seen. I was there for the cigarette story, I don't need to retell it. What I give is something I feel like talking about, something I found strange or funny or interesting. Something that, when I walked away, left me wondering how many truly crazy people are out there. Millions, evidently. Who knows, maybe we're all crazy.

My story has changed a few times through the years, but the one constant is that it's long. You wanna know something, get at the heart of it, you need to sink way down deep. That means details. That means time spent listening, letting it wash over you. Today, for this clerk, it means hearing about Charles.

Charles sat across from me as casually as if we were out for a drink. Right leg crossed over left, hands resting comfortably on the arms of his chair. His face was marked with a fine mist of blood, remnants of the moment his knife sliced through his wife's jugular vein. But it wasn't the blood that made me uptight, or that the crime was so recent, his victim was still warm. It wasn't even the eerie calm of his face. No, what got me were his eyes. Charles had piercing, probing eyes, the kind that sear your skin. The kind of eyes, perhaps, that wouldn't blink as he brutally murdered you. They were a terrifying blue—a striking feature in white people, absolutely mesmerizing in a light-skinned black man. And he just kept staring at me.

Charles and I were in the cramped fourth-floor offices of Atlanta's homicide unit. In an interrogation room, which is nothing more than four walls of battered Sheetrock with a little table and a handful of chairs. He was cuffed and in an orange jumpsuit. His own clothes—the ones soaked with his wife's blood—were stuffed in a paper grocery bag crumpled at his feet.

After a few silent moments, he smiled. "All the angels have been killed," he said. "Did you know that?"

The reason I was there—called out to the homicide offices to sit across from a man who had just stabbed his wife—was because of a detail you can't invent. I have come to believe that truth is stranger than fiction due to the details. Little things our sane and rational mind is unable to dream up. Like, for instance, that stabbing someone is hard work. That no matter how strong you are or how enraged, even deranged, you are, it takes a lot of force to stick a knife into someone's body. Even then, a knife tends to stop when it hits something solid. A rib, for instance. Or a collarbone.

In Charles's fury, he stabbed his wife more than forty times. After two or three slices, the blood, now splattered across his face and soaking through his clothes, really began to flow. That made the knife slick enough that when he struck bone, it slipped. Still he kept stabbing. His fingers were deeply lacerated. And so there I was with a handful of bandages, staring into the blood-splattered face of a man who'd just slaughtered his wife.

"You want me to bandage those fingers for you?"

Charles barely glanced at his hands. "And the angels," he said. "They all had blue eyes."

I set the bandages down. Took a seat across from Charles. "Blue eyes, huh?"

He nodded. "Yup. John Kennedy, November 22, 1963. Robert Kennedy, June 5, 1968. William McKinley, September 6, 1901. Abraham Lincoln, April 15, 1865. John Lennon, December 8, 1980." He looked down at his hands. "Jesus Christ."

"I don't think Christ had blue eyes."

He smiled at me. Then his face turned serious. "She used to look at me, stare at me," he said. "At my eyes."

"Who?"

"The victim." He grunted as he said it, and a strange expression claimed his face. It was the first time he had referred to his wife as the "victim," and it affected him. The look wasn't remorse or hate but surprise. As though he'd been waiting years for her to assume that title, and at last she'd achieved it. "You can wrap my hands now."

It's not every day a killer leans back in his chair so you can stand over him and bandage the wounds he received while disemboweling his screaming wife. My hands shook a bit as I grabbed the gauze and walked around the table. He looked into my face, and I tried with all my strength not to stare at his eyes. As I bandaged his hands, covered in his blood, her blood, the smell filling the room, all I could think was: *I'm next. He's gonna catch me looking. He's gonna think about the Kennedys and Lincoln and Lennon. He's gonna think about Jesus. And he's gonna strangle me.*

I wondered how long it would take a cop to hear me gurgling in the interrogation room. I wondered how long it would take Charles to kill me. I wondered why the cops had left me in here alone for so long. Maybe the cops were wondering that, too, because as soon as I was done, a detective walked in. Charles looked over, nodded, and said, "I know you."

And he did. As he played absentmindedly with the bandages, Charles told the cop he recognized him from TV. He remembered his name. The cop, shocked, looked at me, then back to Charles. As it turned out, Charles had mistaken the detective for his father, who'd also been a cop. But Charles was right about having seen him on TV—the detective's father had been the APD spokesman back in the early eighties, when the infamous Atlanta Child Murders were national news. He'd long since retired, and his son, then only a teenager, had moved up in the ranks and was now the homicide detective standing before us. That Charles had recognized the man from news footage of his father that hadn't aired in over twenty years was a little disturbing.

Would Charles remember me? Would my child someday bump into this man when Charles was old and infirm and paroled because he was no longer considered a threat? Would my child, not knowing his very real and dangerous connection with this man, stare unknowingly into those hypnotic blue eyes and rekindle Charles's long-dormant homicidal delusions?

Probably not. Probably Charles would die in prison and none of us would ever see him again.

Then again, maybe not.

"Anyway, how much do I owe you for the plunger?"

The clerk sniffs as he snaps back to reality. He punches a few buttons, and the price pops up on the screen. He swipes my AmEx. I grab the plunger and head for the door. As I'm leaving, I hear a woman in line say, "Those people have the hardest job."

The clerk has gathered his senses and says, "That's nothing. This one time . . ."

30

Faith Healers

I've been a medic a little over a year. That conversation I had with Chris the day before I took my medic exam—the one when he said I wouldn't kill anyone—seems so long ago. I'm no longer new and untested, no longer scared. I've run enough calls that I can tell the difference between those who think they're dying and those who really are. More important, I know how to handle each. Marty, too, has come a long way, and the two of us have been welcomed into the circle. We aren't merely faces without names. We're Grady medics. And it's now—as we're able to breathe easy, as we're basking in the knowledge that we won't kill anybody—that we manage to do just that.

The call, when it comes, is for a thirty-six-year-old with chest pain. We walk in casually, almost cavalier, and find a guy sweating in an armchair. He's out of breath, nauseated, dizzy, and weak, with the unshakable sense that something bad, something horrible, is about to happen. He is, at this moment, the palest black man on the planet. It doesn't look good. I ask what he's been doing, and he says in between gasps, "Smoking crack."

"How much?"

"Hundred dollars."

I'm not sure how much crack a hundred dollars buys, but if a single rock costs a few bucks, a hundred probably buys a lot. He's young to be having a heart attack, and while we'd be skeptical normally, the crack changes all that. I ask where his pain is, and he says it started as back pain, then slowly burrowed through to his chest and is now trying to eat its way out of his stomach. Think *Aliens*. Think a man about to die.

"You need to come with us."

"Oh, I ain't going to no hospital," he says. Then, taking a deep breath, he asks, "Can't you just give me something right here?"

We continue to badger him. Tell him he's having a heart attack and there's nothing we can do, that he needs to go to the hospital, because if he stays here, he's going to die. His father sits on the couch, unimpressed with the whole situation. The argument continues—the patient won't go, we won't leave him, his father couldn't give a damn—until the patient relents.

"Yeah, I'll go," he says, "but not on that thing." He waves a hand at our stretcher. "I'm a soldier. I'll walk."

His father laughs. Marty laughs.

"Dude, if you wanna walk, walk. I don't care."

We give him some aspirin to chew and walk him out. We're talking away, mostly to each other but to the patient as well. And why not? We're feeling pretty good about ourselves: We did our job and convinced a stubborn man to seek help. We're not paying close enough attention, and by the time we reach the ambulance, our patient is gasping. However bad he looked before, he looks infinitely worse now. It's clear we never should've let him walk. With our help he climbs into the ambulance, plops

down on the stretcher, and dies. I'm looking at him, so I see it—
he tenses, gurgles, then goes limp. Marty has his head turned,
but he hears it. He's standing over the patient. He looks down,
then up at me. "Did he just die?"

"I believe so."

"Oh, fuck."

"Maybe we shouldn't have let him walk."

"Oh, fuck."

We're stunned and just stare, which, it turns out, is no way
to revive even the recently deceased. Finally, a thought passes
between us, vague and slow-moving, a sort of lo-fi telepathy like
rope strung between our tin-can brains—we should go ahead
and do something. Marty drops the head of the stretcher, I rip
off the patient's shirt. Marty fires up the cardiac monitor, presses
the paddles to the man's chest. I jump back an instant before
he presses the shock button and narrowly avoid being shocked.
POP! We turn to the monitor and wait. Wait to see if the shock
worked, if the guy's going to spring back to life, if he's permanently or just temporarily dead. Thankfully, we see it—the tracing of a heart in distress but beating. Beat. Beat. Beat. I grab his
wrist and the pulse is there. Blood is pumping.

What we should be feeling right now is relief. Some things
are clear-cut, and anyone in as much distress as our patient was
when we happily walked him outside never should have been
allowed to walk. Once we convinced him to go, we should've
taken a few extra seconds to convince him to ride. But for us,
that's an afterthought. Less than that. It's a non-thought. I don't
remember walking anybody. What I remember is a man dying
and then, quickly and expertly, the two of us bringing him back

to life. What I feel is pride. We're all smiles. I ask Marty if he wants me to call for fire, get him some help for the ride in, but he shakes his head. "Fuck fire," Marty says. "We saved him once. We can do it twice. Let's just go."

When I step out of the ambulance, his father is waiting, anxious. I tell him his son died, but now he's alive. We brought him back from the dead.

He nods. "Yeah, okay. Look, he's got cigarettes in his pocket," he says, poking his head through the door. "Can you grab 'em?"

"Sir, your son just died. We saved him, but he could die again. We need to hurry. To the hospital."

"But they're right there in his coat pocket."

Our actions are supposed to engender relief or thankfulness. I won't go so far as to say I'm expecting adulation, but hell, maybe I am. Instead, I get a man looking for cigarettes. I shut the door and walk away.

By the time we get to the ER, the patient is talking. He looks a little surprised, his eyes wild from crack and having been dead. He's asking to leave, but the doctors aren't listening. As they wheel him out of the ER and toward the cath lab, the cardiologist tells him to thank us. "These guys saved your life," she says.

The guy looks at us and asks if we've seen his cigarettes. "My dad didn't take 'em, did he?"

And so, yes. We killed someone. But then, with just as much ease, we brought him back to life. This is my first time. Up until this moment, every person I either found dead or who died in front of me has, despite my efforts, remained dead. This is

Marty's second. The first call he ever ran was a guy who dropped while jogging. Just collapsed and died, and Marty, with exactly zero experience, saved him. On his very first try. I realize now that when he said he didn't know anything, when he said he wouldn't be offended if I corrected him, he actually meant it. Because though he doesn't have much experience, he knows, deep down, he's good. The first thing he did on this job was bring the dead back to life. And now, having done it myself, I know just how that feels.

Word has spread, and by the end of our shift, people are talking about it. These people, the ones with more experience, who've been where we are—new and stupid and invincible—they tell us to take it in stride. *Yeah, you saved someone, and that's great,* they say, *but keep some perspective. Don't let it go to your head.*

We nod and say that we'd never do such a thing, but fuck that. We. Are. Good. Coming to the realization of how much power we wield after so much second-guessing and self-doubt—it's intoxicating. Lives are in the balance, and it's just us. Making decisions, pulling the trigger, in control, no one to answer to. Marty has been on the fence about this job, and at times, so have I, but how much cooler can it get than this? The only other person with this much power is a doctor, and being a doctor means getting trapped in a hospital, being surrounded by registration clerks and air-conditioning repairmen and gift-shop teddy bears. We're out roaming the streets, surrounded by feral dogs and people who'd happily do us harm. We're gunslingers.

Though we should listen to the people who've been around, who've stood where we stand, we don't. We take this call to mean exactly what we want it to mean: that the only thing blocking the door between this world and the next is us. Banish all doubt. Tonight and every night from here on out, lives will be saved or not depending on how good we are. We're young and stupid but confident, and we'll gladly tell you God's not dead. He's right here, running calls in the back of an ambulance.

31

Hubris

We're under siege. By the doctors and the fire department and the cops. Not merely outranked in the hospital but overlooked. In the streets we're outgunned, outpoliticked, out on our own. EMS—pulling up the rear in the meat wagon—always comes out on the losing end. But not us. Not anymore.

Marty and I have single-handedly raised the dead and vow, from this day on, that anyone not on this ambulance, not part of this two-man army, is an outsider. They don't understand what we're doing, they aren't operating at our frequency. It's us against the world, and so far as we can tell, we're right. You can't tell us a damn thing.

Our revolt starts immediately and all at once. Most of it, oddly, has nothing to do with patient care, and the little that does has to do with doctors. Those at the top of every food chain exercise their prerogatives, and for doctors, that includes holding everyone below them in at least mild contempt. There are any number of reasons, but somewhere on the list, in all likelihood, is that many doctors started out as nerdy kids who were laughed at and picked on and probably still are, outside of the hospital. Everyone experiences this at some point—being the odd man out—but some people never get over being slighted. Maybe they internalize it, let it fester, until one day, years later, they're a doctor. And there, before them, are dozens of people who aren't. Suddenly, it's revenge of the nerds.

Marty and I get along with a few, but as a group, they're rude and dismissive, aloof to the point of arrogance. We've decided from now on, we'll simply ignore them. There's a handful of drugs and procedures we're allowed to administer only after calling the hospital and discussing it with a physician. We stop doing this. We just proved we know what we're doing, and we figure that if anyone comes around asking why we never bothered to get permission, we'll point to the patient's outcome, which we've already decided will be good. How could it not be? And since the patient will live, since we'll save him, what more can anyone say? How do you argue with the result when the result is a life saved?

That's how we're dealing with the doctors, but we're focused on more pressing matters, more righteous causes. Like pissing off the fire department.

Though we work together—same mission, same calls, same patients—for some reason, medics and firefighters can't get along. The fire guys consider us disorganized, rumpled, undisciplined, lazy, and jaded, while we look at them as dim-witted oafs who geek out on gear while giving poor patient care. In our opinion, they're best suited for the job of ferrying equipment to and from the ambulance. Sure, there are plenty of good firefighters out there, people I've worked with over the years whose arrival in the doorway tells me that things have just gotten easier. But there are others who can't flush a toilet without instructions.

As people, we get along, but as uniformed members of our respective departments, we generally do not. Yet we *have* to work together; we need each other. We exist as two halves of a strange whole, the Israeli-Palestinian conflict in miniature. There is no relief—no way to extricate ourselves long enough to take a deep breath—and so it festers, and everything is a pissing match, a food fight, a shooting war.

Marty and I aren't the only ones. Every Grady medic has stories of firefighters who have bungled patient care or picked fights on-scene. For Marty and me, the issue boiled over at a swimming pool. We were dispatched to a possible drowning and arrived to find a seven-year-old boy on the deck of a public pool, dripping wet, blue, and not breathing. Fire arrived right after we did and must have seen us kneeling over the kid. Or maybe not. It's hard to imagine how they could have seen us, seen what was happening, and then walked away. Which is what they did. The captain grumbled something about this not being their call, and they turned and disappeared. Marty and I were left with the boy. We scooped him up, carried him to the ambulance, and started to ventilate him. After three puffs, the boy jerked upright and vomited a liter of warm stomach water all over Marty. We stood there in shock—with little chewed-up bits of hot dog swimming around the ambulance floor—as the boy gasped and looked around, as shocked as we were.

Though we'd saved him, we'd been abandoned. What if he hadn't started breathing again? What if his heart stopped and he was no longer a kid in need of air but a soon-to-be-dead child in need of CPR? A patient like that requires hands, which is exactly why the fire department is sent out with us. We did our best to raise hell, but the fire department is much more powerful, more politically connected, than EMS, and the chiefs browbeat our supervisors into submission. So we began a low-grade war of retribution. If a call went out in a shopping mall, we'd go over the radio and tell the responding fire crew to enter from the north entrance—even though we were already kneeling over the patient at the south entrance. When they arrived, we'd shrug with surprise as they stomped up, out of breath, having gone half a mile out of their way. Then there was the sauerkraut. We bought a few pounds of it, and every day for a week, we brought it to the same fire station and overcooked it in the same microwave. After two or three days, when we walked in the door, someone saw us and asked what we were cooking. "Some Grady crew's been coming in here, burning sauerkraut," the captain said. "You guys don't have anything like that, do you?" We shook our heads and darted into the kitchen, where Marty threw in the sauerkraut and set the timer to thirty minutes.

But things have changed. We've ascended to a new level. We're above pranking firemen. We're taking our contempt all the way up to the top. One afternoon we're sent to Atlanta Fire headquarters for a dispatcher with difficulty breathing. When we arrive, firefighters are already gathered around her. They have her on oxygen and albuterol and are preparing to give her an IV steroid—all common practices for someone having an asthma attack. Which isn't what is happening. As soon as we walk through the door, we realize the patient is hyperventilating and that the oxygen and the albuterol, not to mention the abrupt introduction of steroids, are only going to make things worse. We push our way in. We cut off the oxygen, yank off the mask. We pull the tourniquet off her arm before anyone can start an IV.

The firefighters are beyond shocked, beyond pissed. We just

plow ahead. Hyperventilation is pretty common, and generally, its cause is psychological. Sometimes a patient gets so pissed—at her husband, her boyfriend, her boss—that she loses her shit. Her breathing picks up until she's dizzy and her vision is starting to dim and her hands are cramping up. Now she can't stop hyperventilating if she wants to, and the situation gets worse and worse until she passes out. Unless someone can calm her. Which is what we do. We talk slowly, so softly that no one else can hear. Marty pushes the crowd of angry firefighters away as I get our patient to breathe in through her nose and out through her mouth. "That's it. Just slow down. You're doing good."

Eventually, she calms down and tells us she just had a fight with her daughter—another eighteen-year-old who's got nothing to learn from the world—and she lost it. She's better now, calm and quiet. We're ready to leave when the fire chief shows up. He's a big man, a full head of hair and a mustache, and he wants us to transport her. This man runs an entire fire department, has thirty years behind him and a couple thousand people below him. He's used to being obeyed. And here are two Grady medics. In his headquarters. Treating one of his employees. And they're looking him in the eye and saying no.

The guy goes through the roof. He's furious, yelling and pointing, making threats, making phone calls. And we couldn't give a damn. We're not firefighters. We're not city employees. We work for Grady; our responsibility is to the patient. Our patient is fine and doesn't want to be transported. We can hear him yelling as we walk out the door. Even as we hop in our ambulance and drive away, it doesn't feel like a coup or a victory. It's simply another call, another job well done. Another patient. We assume it's behind us. Except it isn't. But we don't learn that until later.

• • •

In the meantime, we take our fight to the police. Cops are a nation-state unto themselves, answerable to no one except the mayor, though sometimes they ignore her, too. Many cops operate under the assumption that we're there to whisk their troubles away. They believe that any time they have a person who's a nuisance but not a criminal, it's perfectly acceptable to call an ambulance and have their troubles carted off to Grady. Homeless guy sleeping on the street? Call Grady. Schizophrenic acting up at the Waffle House? Call Grady. Big violent guy who's naked and screaming at passing cars on Fulton Street? Call Grady. And when they do have someone in custody, after they've peppersprayed him or Tased him, or after he's been handcuffed and fallen really, really hard, they want us to come out and certify that he's healthy enough to be transported to jail. These are all minor annoyances, but they're everyday occurrences, and after a while they build up. Especially when you take into account how often we're called out to treat some cop's minor injuries.

Cops scratched on fences? Call Grady. Cops with bruised knees from a minor traffic accident? Call Grady. Cops who've wandered into their own cloud of pepper spray? Call Grady. One afternoon a cop shoots a dog that's bitten him, and we're beaten to the scene by a half-dozen other cops, a police chopper, and a news crew. We're given a police escort back to Grady— they block off every street we cross—where we're met by the head trauma surgeon. All for a cop bitten by a dog. And it's not even a bad bite.

No more. We decide that though we can't stop them from calling us, we'll no longer call them. For anything. Whatever goes down, we can handle it. Shooting, stabbing, fight in progress? We're in. Kicking down doors, wrestling violent psychs, sedating pissed-off meth heads. We're invincible.

For a few months, Marty and I do it all. Everything goes fine until one day it doesn't. We're called out to Bowen Homes for a woman assaulted by her boyfriend. In a city full of housing projects, Bowen Homes is the worst. It's acre upon acre of two-story buildings that spring from the clay like brick mushrooms. It's thousands of people crammed together, the good, the bad, and the violent. It has its own library, its own medical clinic, its own school. Nobody ever sleeps, nobody ever leaves. People are everywhere, at all hours of the night, buying drugs, selling drugs, doing drugs. Some are trying to get by; others are trying to get over. There's noise and chaos, some low-grade ruckus, and *always* smoke drifting up from a hundred smoldering grills.

Marty and I pull in and drive to a dead-end street near the very back of the project. The projects are a beehive, so nothing goes unnoticed. People know what's happened the second it goes down, and as we pull in, people are waving and pointing, showing us the way. We're warned by dispatch that the scene is not safe, but that doesn't stop us. We arrive, get out, walk in, and find a woman beaten unconscious. We take a few minutes to assess her, then load her onto the stretcher and leave. The minute we open the door, all hell breaks loose. At least a hundred people have followed us here, and they're all crowded around the apartment, straining for a look. The girl's family is here, but her attacker is gone, so when they see her—unconscious, bleeding, limp—they have no one to focus their anger on. Except us.

The crowd surges forward. More people are coming, they're screaming, yelling, pushing against the ambulance, against the stretcher. Marty calls for help over the radio, but whether the dispatcher can hear him over this noise, we don't know. The mob is too loud—yelling for us to go faster, to do something, to tell them something. They are distraught and violent, and we're being overrun.

And then, from nowhere, salvation. Three Fulton County marshals—who were serving a warrant in the area and heard our distress call—come speeding over the grass in their cruisers. They're all flashing lights and sirens. They jump out, nightsticks drawn, guns drawn. They're yelling for the crowd to get back and let us through. The crowd goes silent, then parts. We load our patient and back out. We're safe, not because we're good but because we were saved. Because someone else came along and pulled us out of a situation we cavalierly got ourselves into.

That's what breaks the spell. Our arrogance and contempt, our hubris, got us into trouble. Someone else came along and saved us. This is our scariest day on an ambulance, and it ends our brief stint as para-gods. We're brought back to earth, to the real world of two simple medics serving as a single link in the patient-care chain. Unfortunately, our awakening hasn't happened quite quickly enough.

The fire chief—the one we ignored and disrespected and pissed off—has called our supervisors and raised hell. He says we were insubordinate and negligent. He wants something done. The negligence claim soon gets tossed out. It's clear to anyone with any sense that we made the right call. Still, a fire chief is a powerful person. His bruised ego must be dealt with.

So we're told to apologize. Since Marty is the one who spoke to the chief, he's specifically listed in the complaint. The job of apologizing falls on his shoulders alone. He doesn't want to do it. He gets angry and raises his voice as he pleads our case, yelling mostly about the kid by the pool whom we were left to deal with, but about everything else, too. Nobody's listening. Eventually, he composes a handwritten apology and drives to Atlanta Fire headquarters to deliver it in person. He stands alone on the carpet and tells a fire chief that he's sorry. Sorry for disagreeing. Forget that we were right, that the chief's own firefighters dropped the ball and were mishandling a patient. Forget that we came along and saved the day. We stood our ground, and for that we were wrong.

Sorry.

32

Dead on Arrival

Marty is leaving. He says it's partly because of the thing with the fire chief, the betrayal he feels, but also it's the job in general. He says EMS isn't for him and it's time to go.

It's early in the shift, just after sunset. We're in Southeast Atlanta, a few miles from Turner Field, where a few months ago we watched the Braves win the division only to flame out once again in September. We're headed to an abandoned school. There's a cop down here who thinks he's found something but can't be sure—sometimes the eyes play tricks. Right now, though, I'm not terribly interested in this person who's (possibly) dead in an abandoned school. All I can think is that my best friend—the guy I've run calls with and sweated and bled and gotten drunk with—is leaving. Once again I'm going to be alone.

I ask Marty if he's sure. "Because once you leave, that's it," I tell him. "It's over."

"I know."

A fat cop lumbers over, and Marty unrolls his window. The cop tells us he was driving by when a junkie flagged him down and said there was someone inside.

"A body?"

The cop shrugs. His car is parked on the curb, and it's not a regular cruiser but a traffic-enforcement car. "I hand out tickets," he says. "I don't find bodies."

"Where is it?"

The cop hooks a thumb over his shoulder. "In the school, I guess. I'll follow you."

People always talk about how they want to die and at what age, but almost no one considers where. When I die, I'd like it to be peaceful and painless. I'd like it to be quick. But just as much, I'd like it to happen anywhere other than an abandoned building in Southeast Atlanta. A death here isn't merely undignified. It's forgotten. We're crunching through the dead grass, through the weeds and litter, when I ask Marty what he's going to do. "When you leave, I mean."

He shrugs. "Don't know. This job's gotta qualify me for something, right?"

But what? This is what we do, what we've done so many times. Get called out to someone who's not recently dead but truly dead. Dead-and-gone dead. Dead-dead. We've developed a routine for these calls, a system. One of us approaches the family, hands folded, and says, "I'm sorry, but he's dead. Is there someone we can call?" We take turns with the family, but we're both on body detail. We scour the room for answers; we dig through pockets looking for ID, for meds, for clues to what might've happened. We speculate on how long he's been here and why.

One way or another, we'll all be present for this conversation someday.

It's been years since the school was full of children. Though the power has been cut and the windows are boarded up, the chain-link fence has been chewed through and pushed open by junkies and lunatics and bored teenagers. Maybe the odd prostitute. "Well, this should suck," Marty says as we slip through a hole in the chain-link fence and cross the schoolyard on a well-worn path through the weeds. Then: "Scratch that. I changed my mind." I'm expecting him to say he's not leaving, that this strange life is too good to walk away from. Instead he says, "At least he'll be alone. And that's a plus."

Usually, we find them in houses. Most times we find bodies—stiff and swollen—pinned between the toilet and the tub. Even when they're in the bedroom or the kitchen, the bathroom light is on, the medicine cabinet open and rifled through. The dying tend to know something is wrong, and if they can, they make their way to the bathroom. When they never come out, someone knocks and knocks until alarm becomes suspicion becomes anguish becomes a 911 call.

As soon as we enter the school, we're swallowed by darkness. I click on my flashlight and am amazed by its uselessness. This beam of light is our lifeline, what we'll use to get to the body and what we'll use to get out again. Somewhere in the darkness, something moves and I swing my light. We hope it's only a rat, but we're not in here alone.

We shuffle through the auditorium, stepping over fallen pieces of ceiling and piles of turd that dot the floor like a dysenteric minefield. As we go deeper, things get worse. We're in a hallway now, dark as night and shockingly narrow. The plaster ceiling sags and buckles with water damage, long strips hanging down like flypaper. The walls, also plaster, heave forward, lumpy shapeless arms reaching out to grab us as we stumble forward, tripping over debris.

All the while, we can't see. All in a place alive with groans and creaks, the distant moaning of God knows what.

"School, maybe," Marty says.

I stop to shine my light on him. "School?"

"Yeah. Maybe I'll go back to school." The traffic-enforcement officer shuffles his feet at the edge of our small circle of dim yellow light. Marty shrugs. "But maybe not."

We round another corner, and for the first time we catch a whiff of what lies ahead. Decomposition is a terrible, sickly sweet smell, but at least today it tells us we're on the right path. Our trail will end down the next hall. When we turn the corner, we're blinded by a flash of light and immediately stop. We're disoriented from stumbling through the darkness, so it takes a minute to realize what we're looking at—the door at the end of the hall is half glass. My light is bouncing off and shining back in our eyes.

We continue on, the smell more intense with each step, and the traffic cop beside us begins to mumble. Five feet from the door, he says he's never seen a dead body. When we reach the door, the smell is overpowering. Flies as thick as grapes bounce off the glass. It's been over a week, possibly two. It's pure Hollywood—a man in the fetal position, his skin nothing but a roiling bag of maggots. Large sections that should be there simply aren't. When a body is left to nature, words we don't normally associate with humans begin to apply: bloating, rotting, liquefying, bursting. These have all happened. It's the ultimate lesson in humility. We're nothing but meat, and if circumstances allow, we'll end up no different than a possum lying by the roadside.

"I'm just over it," Marty says. "The whole thing." He peeks in the window. "Aren't you?"

The cop groans. He, too, wants out—at least out of this building—but he wandered in without a flashlight, and now he's stuck.

I don't know what else I'd do, and I tell Marty that. "Have you really thought your way through this?"

Marty looks down at his feet but doesn't say anything. He stares at the floor, forehead crinkled like he's deep in thought, but nothing comes. He keeps looking down at the floor, and as his mouth slowly flops open, I realize he's not thinking at all. I shine my light on the ground and there, at our feet, are drag marks. It takes a second to process this information, what the drag marks mean. Then, slowly, I trace them down the hall, back the way we've come. Our patient didn't slink back here to die in peace. He was dragged, perhaps kicking and screaming, to this dark corner of a long-abandoned building and killed. The cop sees what we see. He fidgets with his keys. We've trampled yet another crime scene.

Outside, it's bright. We hop in the truck to write up our short report but have to unroll the windows. There are a lot of things that stay with you when you find the dead. Glasses, canes, clothes, money. A watch that keeps ticking. Today it's the smell. It's sunk into our clothes, our nostrils. It's inescapable.

"So that's it? You've made up your mind?"

Marty nods and that's it. We've come all this way and gone through so much together, from useless and scared to battle-tested, lesson-learned, competent but humble crew. We're exactly where we hoped to be when we set out. How bittersweet it is to have found what we've been looking for, only for it to be dead on arrival.

Two months later, Marty's gone.

Poof.

I'm left to wonder why I'm still here. Did I choose to stay, or was I left behind? Maybe I like it here, have decided this is where I belong, that nothing else could ever compare to rushing through the streets to perform, to witness, and occasionally, to save. But maybe not. Maybe I have nowhere else to go and I was, in fact, left behind. Sitting in the back of the ambulance, staring at a succession of patients—always the same complaint, always the same place—I start to get angry. I start to get bitter. I really begin to hate this job. I've been warned it could happen someday, and now someday is here.

All I can do is hold on tight, because the burnout's coming, and it's a long drop to the bottom.

BOOK FOUR

The Fall

33

Swirling the Drain

Early on a Sunday morning, I go looking for a priest. It's late November, cold and raining. As soon as I went in-service, dispatch sent me to a Spanish-speaking trailer park in Southeast Atlanta. I'm here now, looking for the priest because he speaks English, but he's too busy to talk. I can see him, way up ahead of me, but I can't go after him; anyway, he's surrounded by an enormous crowd. It's a parade, really, and he's leading it. Somewhere in the middle is a grandmother, yelling to no one, carried along by the slow procession of mourners weaving its way through the trailer park to the shuffle of weary feet.

So we wait and sit quietly over a child covered ominously by a sheet. We're waiting for the inevitable screech of tires, for the wail of a mother who isn't sure but suspects the worst. A mother who doesn't speak English and whom we can't let in the ambulance, not without warning her. Suddenly, a commotion. Without being told, we know she's here, and right then I hope someone tells her quickly—she deserves that, at least. But the priest is still up there, still surrounded, the parade still marching on toward nothing. Telling her falls to me.

I jump out of the ambulance and try to calm her, slow her down, explain that there was nothing we could do, nothing anyone could do. But she's beyond all that, and my words of condolence are delivered in a language she doesn't speak. I look around frantically for help, and there sits a nine-year-old. She's waiting for the bus, Hello Kitty backpack slung over her shoulder, juice box and Pop-Tart in her lap. I ask if she knows this woman, if she's the mother. The girl nods. I do the only thing I can. I tell the girl to say what I say, to be gentle but direct, to use my exact words. "Say the baby has died. Don't say *gone* or *passed* or *no longer with us*." These words are confusing and, to the hopeful mind of a mother, cruelly misleading, as if her child isn't dead but somewhere else. The girl turns to the mother and, in a voice both clear and steady, delivers the news.

The sky comes crashing down.

It's been a bad year.

After Marty left, I slipped into a funk. I don't want to be here, and worse, I don't want to be with the person seated next to me. *Whoever* it is. Marty's slot has been left open, so I no longer have a regular partner but a succession of part-timers and misfits. Of the people who regularly rotate through my truck, I get along with one, and he, naturally, is here the least. Usually, it's one of the others, none of whom is any good. For a while I tried to get along, and when that failed, I started to argue. Then I stopped caring. Now I'm riding out the year in silence.

Oddly, the crash of my professional world coincides with the crash of the economy. It takes a while for the havoc loosed on the rest of the country to reach Atlanta, but when it does in 2008, it comes as a shock to a city that has been in the midst of a historic decades-long expansion. Back in the early eighties, Atlanta went from tiny Southern town to international city almost without warning. The city sprang up from itself in all directions, sprawling across an enormous swath of North Georgia. At one point Atlanta was growing at a faster rate than any city ever had.

Initially, the growth was suburban, but then came the Olympics and a nationwide resurgence in urban development. It became fashionable to live in the city, and neighborhoods were gentrified and rebuilt. Thousands upon thousands of condo units went up. Home values shot up the way they did everywhere, and people overpaid by a mile for every square foot of city living.

And now the market has crashed. People are losing their jobs and losing their houses, and all the foreclosures are leaving brand-new multi-story condos either empty or half-filled with renters. The people who remain, the ones who bought at overinflated prices and can't get out from under the debt, stay until the bitter end. They pawn their furniture and wait for the lights to be turned out. Maybe they were raised soft and aren't prepared for hard times or have too much pride to work a low-paying job. One day the phone rings and it isn't a friend or even a bill collector but the bank. "We're taking the house," they say. "The Fulton County marshals will be there in the morning to serve the eviction notice. Please be dressed."

Unprepared for a life without comforts—unable to let go, hit bottom, and rebuild—they call 911 and say they're considering suicide. Death threat before dishonor.

The first of these runs I make takes me to the eleventh floor of a sparkling-new—and eerily empty—high-rise in the heart of midtown. It's been a long week, a long month, and there's no end in sight. We get off the elevator at the eleventh floor and walk down the silent hall and into an empty condo. It isn't just empty but barren. There's no furniture, no pictures, no dishes, nothing except a TV mounted on the wall. The cable has been disconnected and the cord hangs limp, a three-and-a-half-foot coaxial reminder of everything that no longer is. Our patient leans against the island, absently shuffling through a stack of letters explaining why the power or water or electricity was cut. There's a summons to appear in court on charges of check fraud. Faced with piling bills and an empty bank account, she started writing bad checks for groceries and let a tough situation go criminal. There's a cell phone on the counter, sitting in a pink cover dotted with rhinestones, the lone hint of a better, more decadent time in this otherwise white and solitary place. The phone's on speaker, and her father, back in Florida, details the situation to a cop who got here a few minutes before we did.

After her eviction notice arrived, our patient called 911 and said she was going to swallow all the Tylenol she could find and wait out the end. She went to the bathroom, opened the bottle, and tipped it over her mouth. Nothing came out. It was gone, just like everything else. Now she says she's changed her mind and wants to stay home, but once you say the word *suicide*, suggest it, even hint at it, you're going. There's no backing away, and this is what the cop is telling her father. When I tell our patient to gather up her belongings, her lips curl into a smile. There's nothing left except the summons. I pick it up, stuff it ceremoniously back in its envelope, and slip it in her coat pocket. She leaves her apartment without a fight.

The calls continue like this, one after another, as the bills stack up and people weigh their narrowing options. It gets to the point that every time I see a foreclosure notice, I wonder what's going on inside and whether the people living there have resolved to tough it out and rebuild or if they, too, will be carted off in the back of an ambulance.

Not everyone merely threatens suicide.

There's a man who sits behind his closed door with a pistol. When the marshals arrive to evict him, he cocks the hammer, swallows the gun, and pulls the trigger. There's a woman who shoots herself in Piedmont Park whose body is found the next morning by joggers. One woman drops a month's worth of medicine—dozens of giant horse pills popped loose from blister packs—into a blender. She turns it into a slurry and downs the whole thing. I don't know what kind of death she had, but when we arrive, she's blue and bloated on the couch, a long, angry suicide note at her side. Then there's the teenager who hangs himself from a tree in his front yard. His dangling body is so eerie and grotesque—a horror film at the break of dawn—that none of us thinks to knock on the door until his startled grandfather wanders out to stand beside us.

Some people try suicide and fail. Some fake suicide and fail at that, too. This last kind, the unconvincing fakers, we find alive, angry, flopped out on the floor in their own approximation of a death pose.

It's raining when we pull up to the house—a split-level ranch built in the seventies as part of an ambitious in-town development that, long ago, lost even the pretense of promise. The whole area has been left to whoever will claim it, in this case a family of five unruly girls and their aging and eternally put-out grandmother. The front steps are cracked, the railing has rusted and been bent out of shape, and the yard is nothing but a bowl of wet clay. The driveway is hidden beneath three abandoned cars waiting patiently for help that will never come. I pull up my jacket hood as I step out into the rain. A pack of young girls—frantic and beyond consolation—scrambles down the steps, screaming that their sister has killed herself.

I nod. "Where is she?"

They point toward a set of narrow and unlit stairs. An old woman meets us at the bottom; unlike everyone else in the house, she's calm. My partner and I wait, in this very small hallway, for this very old woman to speak. After a few seconds, she spits a stream of tobacco juice into a plastic cup and opens a bedroom door. Inside there's nothing but dirty laundry and old take-out boxes, never vacuumed carpets, the Sheetrock marinated in decades of mildew and smudged brown by dirty hands. At the far end of the room, our patient is flopped out on a sheetless queen-sized bed. There are roaches everywhere. The old woman shoots out another stream of tobacco juice and says our patient, motionless on the bed, has gone and killed herself again.

"Again?"

"Yup."

My partner picks his way over and takes a look. I turn to the old woman, but before I can say a word, she sums up our patient's life as a series of bad decisions punctuated by the occasional suicide. By now my partner has assessed our patient and found her to be alive and merely faking death. Our attention can be turned to the tricky art of raising the dead.

There are a number of ways to do this, none medical. Sometimes I use shame. Perhaps the patient, feeling underappreciated, has gone limp during Easter Mass, slithered out of her pew and died, rather auspiciously, under Jesus's watchful eye. Sometimes just mentioning how much stress this has placed on Nana's aging heart will bring her back. Other times I'll flick the eyelids or squeeze the fingertips between a pen and my thumb. If the faker is truly hard-core, I'll slide an airway device into the right nostril, which tends to wake her in dramatic fashion—think Uma Thurman in *Pulp Fiction*.

Before I can decide, the old woman shoots a stream of tobacco juice through her front teeth. "There's usually a suicide note," she says.

Well, I'll be damned. I scan the dresser, the nightstand, the floor. No note. I step back and take a good look at the patient, who's on the bed, eyes closed, mouth open. Her left arm extends at an unnatural angle, pointing toward a shelf. Sure enough, that's where I find the note.

I grab it and crouch beneath the one working light and start reading. It's a train wreck. Bad penmanship, misspellings, run-on sentences, non-sentences—the whole thing is an unintentional non sequitur. Finally, we reach the how. In bold script accented by a large arrow pointing toward the shelf, the note reads, *And so I swallowed these bullets and them pills.*

I scramble across the bed and find four Tylenols and three .22-caliber bullets. It should be mentioned that a .22 doesn't shoot large bullets. We aren't talking shotgun shells. The dreaded .22 fires a bullet the size of the little red eraser on the end of a pencil. Even with the shell casing, it's smaller than a cashew. The old woman laughs.

But there's real work at hand now. Tylenol seems like a very innocent drug, so it's a common choice for young girls looking to punish a boyfriend or a parent. *I'll just take a few of these,* the girl says to herself as she swallows twenty Tylenols, *and then they'll be sorry.* And someone *will* be sorry, all right. Too much Tylenol kills the liver. Slowly. And painfully. The ones lucky enough to be found in time can look forward to a rather painful and brutal process called a stomach lavage. The others can look forward to a slow and unnecessary death.

My partner dumps the contents of the bottle on the bed. The pill count printed on the label is twenty-five, and we find eighteen. Subtract the four removed for demonstrative purposes and our patient has taken a total of three tablets. Now we all laugh.

Still our patient feigns death. I read on. More finger-pointing, accompanied by more snickering from the old lady. At the bottom, our patient has signed her name—illegibly—and has been courteous enough to include a P.S. This addendum piques my curiosity. What kind of insight is so important that it has to be included in the suicide note but is trivial enough to be excluded from the main text? I read it aloud. " 'Nook Nook will always be in my heart.' " I lower the note. "Who the hell is Nook Nook?"

The old woman says, "Nook Nook was a real jackass. Used to live down the street."

I ask how he passed, and she says he didn't. He moved to Charlotte.

There you have it. The wisdom of our age knows no bounds. I toss the note and crawl across the bed. I reach out, lift the dead woman's wig, and tell her we've had enough, that you can't die from swallowing bullets or taking three Tylenols. I say her family's concerned and would be delighted to hear that she's fine. "The game is up. You're alive and we all know it. Open your eyes."

And she does.

34

Grand Theft Auto

I'm not sure what day it is, what month, what year. Though I'm not happy now, I know I was once, that I had a good partner. We were friends and I even liked the job. I was good at it. I know all this only because I still feel the absence. I've been adrift so long that someone pulls me aside in Grady and asks with sincerity: "What the hell's happened to you? You don't look good. Are you okay?"

No. I'm angry and miserable and I almost don't even care. I'm burned out.

The late nights and early mornings. The misery of working through the sticky swelter of a Georgia summer and the icy chill of a wet Southern winter. Working weekdays and weekends, the indescribably painful hours spent staring at a windshield when you know everyone you love is at home celebrating Christmas. Grumpy nurses, arrogant doctors, shitty partners—oh, the *parade* of shitty partners—and the sharp smell of urine cleaned with bleach.

And all this before the patients.

The sick ones who will die because of a mistake you made or, more often, because it was their time to go and your time to watch. The unsick ones who whine and complain and call 911 for a toothache or a headache or a cut on the finger, knowing full well the bus driver demands payment up front while the ambulance will send a bill they can ignore.

Like a recurring dream, every working day holds the same frustrations, and the working days never change, they just stretch out for all eternity. For months I've wondered how it will end. Maybe I'll reach my limit and quit. Maybe, like so many others, I'll ruin my back carrying an enormous woman down stairs she had no business climbing in the first place.

I'm tired of the patients, tired of the job, tired of everything. I float from partner to partner for a year, and then relief. A new partner. A good one who could bring me back from the brink, but he's in medic school and quickly upgrades, sending me back into the rotation. Before the start of every shift, I drive to work hoping I'll get someone good, but just before I get to Grady, as I'm pulling off the highway and into the city, my stomach drops and the nausea sets in because I know I won't. I know I'll get someone who hates the job or hates the patients or loves it all but isn't competent. Every day it's partner roulette. I show up praying the barrel will spin to an empty chamber, but I always draw the live round.

It goes like this forever.

All that anger and frustration is bubbling to the surface. I'm no longer merely burned out. Tonight I've drifted over the double-yellow line separating burnouts from Killers. I'm standing in a high-rise, peering through the blue haze of a two-decade-old pack-a-day habit, watching a man slowly gasp, pitch forward, and slump to the floor. The call came out for a patient complaining of a sudden onset of confusion. We drove over, parked out front, and walked in. His apartment was on the top floor, fourteen stories up, so we should've brought everything. But this building, even this apartment, is the origin of a thousand bullshit calls. I've been here too many times to count, and it's never, *never,* what they say it is. Except tonight. And now I'm standing here empty-handed, fourteen stories and a long elevator ride from my ambulance, from my equipment. And the patient is dying.

When we walked in, he was sitting up. He looked at us, eyebrows raised, and nodded. Before I could say a word, he was out of his chair and facedown on the floor.

"Grab him! Grab him!"

My partner is slow-moving, the kind of guy who never recognizes a situation has gone to hell and it's time to hustle. I drop to my knees and check for a pulse. The man has one, but he's not breathing. I grab the jump bag, yank out the BVM, and give him two quick puffs of room air—the oxygen tank is sitting happily outside in our ambulance. We grab him by the wrists and ankles and toss him on the stretcher. I do another quick check for a pulse and, finding one, start pushing him toward the door.

We know nothing about this guy. Not what's going on, his meds, history, anything about his complaint, even his name. We know he was confused and now he isn't breathing.

"Get his meds, his wallet, whatever," I shout at my partner. "Anything you can find."

He returns with no meds, just a wallet and a checkbook.

"Son of a— Come on, man."

I hand him the BVM and run to the kitchen, open the fridge, and find some half-empty insulin vials. In the bedroom I find a couple empty pill bottles, some discharge papers. I snatch it all and we're out the door. I'm scared. Scared that he'll die and it'll be our fault. I'm nothing but a trembling wreck, face flushed, mouth dry, a set of wide, terrified eyes.

By sheer luck, his heart waits until we reach the ambulance to stop. For whatever reason, the fire department never shows up, so it's just us, struggling to catch up but never quite getting there. At the hospital, they pronounce him dead and that's that. Outside the ER, after it's over, I sit on a bench while my partner cleans the ambulance. This has all the earmarks of a patient who simply had the Big One; there was probably nothing we could have done about it. But the fact remains that I got lazy and in-different and showed up unprepared. What if he'd died in his apartment? What if we'd needed our equipment but didn't have it because I'd left it fourteen floors below?

I spend a few days sitting around and wondering if this is my cue to leave—if I've turned, like two-day-old meat left out of the fridge, and if it's irreversible. *Is there time to salvage this thing?* I'm still thinking it over a few shifts later when, out of nowhere, someone steals my ambulance.

Really, it couldn't have come at a better time. People always say they're waiting for a sign, and here, in big bold letters, is mine. We're dispatched to a third-floor condo to see a patient with difficulty breathing. We grab the equipment but don't lock the ambulance doors, which may sound strange, but I've never heard of *anyone* locking the doors. Ever. So we go upstairs, begin treatment, load the patient onto the stretcher, and bring him down. We walk through the lobby, nod to the doorman, and get outside to find our ambulance gone. Really gone. Vanished.

"What the fuck . . ."

I stand on the curb, mouth open, lips slowly curling into a smile, while my partner runs up and down the block as if it'll be there, as if it hasn't been stolen but simply hidden. Even the patient knows it's gone. It's late—three in the morning—and here we are, two lonely medics pushing a stretcher down a dark street.

The phone picks up on the sixth ring. Across town, our supervisor is huddled in her office, feet up on the desk, phone cradled between her ear and shoulder. Her voice sounds groggy, like she's been asleep, like this is the last conversation she wants to have.

"You're not gonna believe this," I say.

"Try me," she says.

"My ambulance has been stolen."

"Great."

"I'm serious."

"It's too late for this."

"I know."

"So quit fucking around."

"I'm not."

"You're not?"

"I'm not."

Our supervisor shows up, the police show up. Another ambulance is dispatched to transport our patient. We're sent back to Grady to fill out departmental incident reports. My partner is panicking. I'm almost happy. I've wanted this to be over for so long.

A few hours later, while our fate is being mulled over, the police find our ambulance. It was driven across town and abandoned in a vacant lot, keys in the ignition, gas in the tank. For some reason, before the thief left, he whipped out his dick and pissed all over the cab. He got the dash, the steering wheel, both seats, the radio. The absurdity never ends.

That morning I sleep better than I have in months. It's exhaustion, yes, but also the knowledge that it's over. Finally. The next night I shower, put on a fresh uniform, and show up at work to have my sentence read. But no one mentions the ambulance. Ever. Not the cops, not the supervisors, not the unlucky medic who had to mop up all the piss. Certainly not the guy who stole it. It's the crime that was never committed.

Imagine my disappointment.

35

Mold Them in Your Image

After my stolen ambulance has been found, after it's back on the road and no longer smells like urine, after I've endured the embarrassment of a local news cycle, I'm named an unofficial field training officer. Grady's turnover rate is enormous, worse than ever, and they can't keep people on the streets. Nor can they get new ones in fast enough. We're getting a dozen new hires a month, too many for the current FTOs to handle. They need more, but there's no time to go through the process—the applications, the testing, the interviews—so the existing FTOs get together and suggest a handful of experienced medics. People who've been around, who are good at their jobs, who have the respect of their peers. To my shock, I'm among those mentioned.

The night before the start of my workweek, the phone rings. It's the director of training. Even though I haven't applied, even though I'm visibly and all but irreparably burned out, he says I'd make a good FTO.

"Are you interested?" he asks.

I accept the job without hesitation.

My first new hire is from New York, with years of experience, and this should be easy for her. A quick three weeks to prove she won't kill anyone and then off on her own. It should be nothing more than a rubber stamp. It should be relaxing. It's a complete failure. She doesn't know the protocols, can't handle patients, can't handle pressure, can't hustle, can't multitask—can't function as a medic.

At the end of the first week, someone from training asks how she's doing.

"Terrible," I say. "Worse than terrible. That she hasn't killed anyone yet is sheer luck."

I go home that night, expecting her to be taken off my bus and given to someone else. Instead, they double down and saddle me with a brand-new EMT as well. Now I have two new hires, both clueless, both looking to me for help. We're pitiful. Things reach a boiling point one day when we're busy as hell and calls are dropping back to back. The EMT can't drive, and the medic can't tell him where to go. She's buried beneath a pile of paperwork, he's sweating and wobbly and complaining about missing lunch. Then we run a patient with low blood sugar who's barely conscious and totally pissed off. The medic doesn't know what to do; I'm running around the room, trying to keep the EMT from punching the family and the medic from giving the wrong medication. Any time I focus my attention on one, the other starts fucking something up behind me.

I take over and tell them both to watch, which they're all too happy to do. The second we clear that call, we catch another, and on the way, the two of them get so lost and are screaming so loudly at each other that I have to force them to pull over so I can get behind the wheel. When we finally arrive on-scene, the EMT slips and falls and knocks himself out.

Three weeks have never dragged on so slowly.

My parade of newcomers continues. Grady is a kind of mecca in the world of EMS, a destination job because of the volume and the reputation. There's always new blood, it's just not necessarily the right blood. There are realities to working at Grady that medics don't face anywhere else. Like breaking into abandoned buildings or helping a cop search the grass for the pistol used to kill your patient. There are other obstacles, with respect not just to Grady but to public hospitals in general. Like not having what you need when you need it.

"He says I have to pay." I'm on the phone with a supervisor again. This time I'm not on the street but in a gas station.

"Excuse me?"

"He says if I don't pay, I can't leave."

I'm at a Citgo on Bankhead Highway, leaning against the counter, smiling politely to the clerk while whispering into my phone. On the other end is a supervisor who has other things she'd rather be doing than dealing with my gas situation.

"He won't let you leave?" she asks.

There's a problem with our fuel cards. Someone hasn't paid the bill, and they're not working. They haven't worked in a couple of days, so we're operating on good faith. Gas stations are letting us fill up and keeping a tally; they know exactly how much gas we've pumped and what we owe them. That number is getting high. And this gas station owner out here on Bankhead has decided he's done extending credit.

"He says a whole bunch of units have come in—"

"Five," the clerk says. "Five."

"Five units have come in and not paid for gas. He wants to get paid. Now."

"Okay, tell him I'll be right there."

I tell the clerk, "My supervisor's coming."

"Fine," the clerk says. "But you wait."

Into the phone, I say, "He wants me to wait."

My supervisor is getting annoyed. She starts to rail on about how much money we spend at his place, how I'm an emergency vehicle, not only expected but mandated by state law to respond to any and all emergencies in my zone.

"Tell him you're leaving," she says.

"He said if I walk out the door, he'll call the cops."

"For what?"

"Theft."

My supervisor laughs. "You gotta be shitting me."

"I don't believe I am."

"Just run," she says. "Go."

I'm halfway through the store before the owner realizes I'm actually gonna run out. There are other patrons in here, watching this. I wonder what they're thinking as I burst out the door. Behind me, I hear the clerk's voice, angry and high-pitched. I hear the beep-boop-boop of his phone as he calls 911. I'm running across the parking lot, yelling for my new hire to start it up and put it in gear. Behind me, I hear footsteps and yelling. The ambulance is moving when I reach the door, and I hop along with it, door open, and swing myself in. We bump over the curb and rattle away down the road. Just a couple of petty thieves in a City of Atlanta ambulance.

My new hire is white as a ghost, and after a minute he asks if we just stole gas.

"Yes."

"Is that normal?" he asks.

"How do you define normal?"

36

The Stork Rides Again

And then there's all the vagina.

Where once I was down and all but beaten by this job, I'm back—buoyed by the excitement of my new hires—and for that I'm rewarded with an unending line of pregnant women. Not just pregnant but in labor. This year I've delivered more babies than any medic alive and have earned the Stork Award. For twelve months I see more vaginas than I'm prepared for. Many more, but then I'm not given a choice. They simply come at me. The first time a woman, stripped naked to the waist, flung her legs apart and demanded I get in there to see what was happening, I was understandably taken aback. Eventually, they become routine, another body part in need of attention.

Most years, deliveries are rare calls. This year they're seeking me out, tigers slowly and methodically cutting off my escape routes until there's nothing left but to walk right to them. Some medics go their entire career without delivering a single child. This year my career total hits thirteen.

They've found me at a strange time, all these vaginas and the babies emerging from them. My wife is pregnant with our first child, one of a thousand babies scheduled to be born this year. We were told more than once that pregnancy might not be in the cards for us. For many pregnant women—definitely the ones who deliver in an ambulance—conception is the easy part. They've often accomplished that task accidentally, sometimes unknowingly. Not us. We've endured years of fertility treatments, including multiple failed in utero and in vitro fertilization attempts. The growing swell of my wife's belly—the presence we fear might fade away without a sound—represents tens of thousands of dollars, an uncountable number of ultrasounds and doctors' visits, intrusive exams, pills, shots, and our own fluctuating hopes.

Over and over we tried, and then one day Sabrina was pregnant. In vitro attempt number three worked. So began nine months of analyzing every dizzy spell, every cramp and unexpected movement, for signs that something—*anything*—was happening. People tell me that being in medicine and knowing about the human body is a good thing. It's not. Knowing what *could* happen—having seen it, how it affects people—is not good. There are truths I'd rather not know.

During the years-long process—our reproductive wilderness years—I believed, maybe without real conviction, that the worries would end once Sabrina was pregnant. But as any parent can attest, fears are only amplified once a child ceases to be theoretical and becomes a living, breathing, gestating possibility.

First Trimester

The first miscarriage I worked was the worst. Tiny hands, fully formed, curled into fists that dangled from arms attached to the world's smallest human. Nobody told me it would be like this. I imagined blood and pain and a quiet woman. Instead, we got a person in miniature, asleep in the Tupperware. At first our patient wanted to hold him, then didn't and placed him on the stretcher. We hit a bump and the container fell off. He landed in the street, as soft as a raindrop. The process of picking him up and finding a suitable place to carry him was funereal—imagine two ashamed pallbearers in the orange glow of a streetlight.

Most times it's not that dramatic. Often first-trimester problems arrive as a presentiment—an anonymous voice from deep inside the body, whispering that something might have gone wrong. Sometimes there's blood, sometimes not. Many women know, though they might not be able to put a finger on how. All too often it's not a miscarriage, only morning sickness or cramps or back pain, the dizziness that creeps in from dehydration and exhaustion. These women, the ones who call every day for the duration of the pregnancy, have stacks of unfilled prescriptions and discharge paperwork from last month, last week, last night. Their paperwork is nothing but admonishments—direct and not at all subtle—*not* to return to the hospital, *not* to call 911. But still these women call. And we take them.

Second Trimester

It happened on a normal day. We were dispatched to the far end of town for a woman with abdominal pain. She was pregnant and bleeding in her apartment. When we walked through the door, she didn't speak. Her mother was there and said she was twenty-three weeks pregnant. When we reached the back of the ambulance, she yelled that something was coming. In went the stretcher with us behind it. I yanked her pants off. The doors were open. There was no time. There, in full view of the world, she delivered a tiny, lifeless child onto the stretcher. She was panting and nervous, asking how he was doing. The words *uh, well, not good* shouldn't have to be the first thing a new parent hears. We clamped the cord and cut it, wrapped him in a blanket, and placed him on his back. He wasn't breathing, had no heartbeat. We suctioned his mouth and tried to stimulate him. Nothing. I began chest compressions, using a single finger on his tiny chest. We tried to ventilate him, but our equipment was too big. We were twenty minutes from nowhere, an eternity when you have something too small for any of your equipment. Never had a situation felt so hopeless.

We arrived at the hospital with a nervous mother and a child that never was. Then, as we pulled the stretcher out of the ambulance, a change. His heart started to beat, big and bounding, each beat visible through his translucent skin. It continued—the outsize thumping of his awakened heart—through the parking lot, down the hall, into the elevator, and beyond that to the neonatal intensive-care unit. An anxious pack of nurses and a single doctor awaited our arrival. They instantly washed over both mother and child like a crashing wave.

It's difficult, if not impossible, to track the progress of one among thousands, so what happened to the kid after that, I don't know. He disappeared into the health-care ocean without leaving so much as a ripple. What I know is what I knew that day: that a tiny child no bigger than a soda bottle, born in a parking lot, whose life began among the dead, had a chance. I know, too, that it was our last call of the day. We went back to the hospital, turned in our equipment, and went home. I stripped off my clothes, showered, put on jeans and a T-shirt. I poured a drink, cooked dinner, ate, watched television, and went to bed, all the while thinking, *What a strange, strange job.* The next morning I awoke and went back to work.

Third Trimester

At thirty-seven weeks, the whole world changes. Time has sneaked up on us—Sabrina is full-term—and that very *large* swell in her belly is no longer a possibility, or a fetus, really, but a child.

It's around this time that conversation among our friends turns to the possibility of an accidental home delivery and how, unlike the thousands of unfortunate Americans who unexpectedly find themselves delivering an infant in the backseat of a car, I, at least, will be prepared. Someone suggests that I steal an OB kit from work and keep it at home in case of the unthinkable. Sabrina makes it clear that she doesn't want me to even *see* what's happening at the moment of delivery, let alone participate. I don't consider home delivery an option. Again the curse of experience. I've seen mattresses destroyed and car seats, comforters, couches—entire carpets—rendered unusable. I've witnessed the horrified fathers and the confused dogs and the pain of a natural childbirth. I know the unmentionable reason why expectant mothers are given enemas in the hospital.

Near the end I fret over every detail, the biggest of which is *where*. We're lucky in Atlanta to have Northside Hospital, a baby factory known for churning out more children than any facility in the country. Many expectant mothers plan out every detail of what's to come. But sometimes nature writes a different script, and the child is welcomed into the world by two medics crouched on the dining room carpet. We come dressed in goggles, gloves, and a gown and offer nothing but an OB kit containing a blue bulb syringe, cord clamps, a disposable scalpel, sterile gauze, a foil blanket, and a pink and blue skullcap. Often the pain gets to be too much, and when that happens, two firemen whom the woman doesn't know will throw her legs over their shoulders as I yell for her to push and the husband, pale white and withering, leans against the wall.

Sometimes a home birth was the plan all along.

One night I walk into a barely furnished apartment vibrating with the thud of tribal drums, slow and rhythmic like giants marching. In the back bedroom, I find a woman standing in an inflatable pool filled knee-high with water. In the corner, a naked woman stands with her legs spread, umbilical cord trailing down to an infant lying on the floor between her feet. They have attempted a water birth—some strange claim to a tradition and ancestry they clearly didn't understand. They got the date right but screwed up the execution, so the child has spent six minutes underwater. Nobody seems to fully grasp the significance of what they've done except us and perhaps the child, but it's too late for him.

Sabrina's water breaks at two A.M. She went to see her doctor earlier in the day, and they agreed that if nothing happened by Friday, she'd be induced. All those plans are out the window. She calls to me from the bathroom, and despite being in a deep sleep, I recognize the tone of her voice and jump out of bed.

We've already packed a bag, so there's nothing to do but get dressed and head out the door. I desperately want to leave, to start driving, to get out of the house and into the hospital. Baby number one typically takes the longest to deliver, with subsequent deliveries getting easier and faster. But it's all so subjective, so dependent on factors beyond our control, that I just want to *get there*. Sabrina insists on covering the car seat with a bath towel, and once it's down, I drive like hell.

Even though her water has broken, there are no contractions, no urge to push, and we're able to enjoy the moment. Something big is happening—a forever kind of thing—and this moment, the two of us in the car with a bath towel, is the beginning. It's hard not to smile. There's nothing to do but wait.

And that's what we do. *Wait*. Without end, without progress. It takes hours for the contractions to kick in and hours more for everything to get real. Finally, there's a spinal tap, an epidural, more exams, more waiting. The frequency of contractions, like a slow burn, picks up little by little until we almost don't notice the moment has arrived. Suddenly, there are nurses and a doctor, and for the first time everyone is wearing a gown. All I can think is *I'm not ready for this, I'm not ready for this.* The doctor asks if I want to help, and even as I say yes, my hands are trembling.

When the doctor tells me to step around to the end of the bed, Sabrina is deep into what will be the final push. As I get close, the head appears. I reach down, cradle it, and guide it out. Nothing dramatic, nothing to report. No disaster. Merely a child, a son. Healthy and here and ours.

By technicality, his delivery is number fourteen.

37

The Summons

I was told years ago that if I stuck with this job long enough, three things would happen: First, I'd burn out and need to find my own way back. Second, with time, I'd run every call I ever hoped to run. And third, I'd end up in court. The first two have already happened, though I never expected the third. Until I got sued.

When news of the lawsuit arrives—alleging that I'm a poor provider who irreparably harmed someone with my negligence—I'm not surprised. I remember the patient. I knew this was coming. Though it was a few years ago now, the details of that day are clear and simple. Basically, it unfolded like this.

So I've known this day was coming. I've known—at least *suspected*—that a lawyer has been creeping around the doors of my past, looking for a way in. There's been nothing to do but wait for him to pick the lock and steal inside. Now it has happened. It's early spring, and I walk into work to find a letter shoved in my mailbox. It's from the hospital's lawyers, and they're asking, almost apologetically, if I can set aside some time to speak—when it's convenient, of course. I schedule a meeting, arrive at their offices, shake hands, sit down, and am stripped to the bone.

Every detail of the call is dissected until its parts no longer look like they belong to the same whole. My recollection is put on trial and sentenced to death prior to its conviction. After several hours, I explain that I have to leave, that I have a child back home who's a few weeks old, and my wife works in the morning.

---

1 The terms of the suit, at least the very few shared with me, stipulate that I'm not to speak about the details of the call.

This inquisition is over. The attorneys look at each other and, because I've left them without a choice, say I can leave. I stand.

"Do you have any questions for us?" one of the attorneys asks. She's bone-thin, and her jacket hangs limp from her shoulders. Her partner is powerfully built but says almost nothing.

"Am I being sued?"

"No."

Relief. Because the hospital has bigger pockets, I'll merely serve as witness at my own trial.

A month later, we meet again. This time with less cross-examination. More questions.

"Give shorter answers," the attorney says, shrugging off her jacket to reveal a set of skinny arms. "No unsolicited explanation. Make them work for it."

The whole thing is a sucker punch. It's unnerving to be drilled and doubted and accused of the worst while never having a chance to explain. The facts are an afterthought; what matters is how each side can manipulate and present them. I develop a nagging nausea, like the faint echo of food poisoning that lingers for days after the purging. I'm embarrassed and isolated from everything, even my own confidence. Imagine being exiled from your mind.

But I'm not alone. My old partner, the one who was there that day, is going through the same thing. We're kept separate, never interviewed together, discouraged from speaking to each other about what happened that day and how, years later, it's all playing out. I suppose, from the outside, this seems perfectly acceptable, but in EMS, where your partner is not merely your lifeline but the entirety of your world for the forty minutes you're running a call, to be split up is completely unnatural. Especially when you're friends. We ran God knows how many calls together. For years we laughed, sweated, and drifted off to sleep in the back of an ambulance. We shared our dreams and insecurities, our dinner. We did CPR on a woman in her own kitchen as her indifferent family watched television. He's from South Georgia and huge, a giant in EMS blue who, through sheer physical intimidation, once got us out of a very dangerous situation.

The waiting lasts forever.

The deposition does not. If you provide a common complaint and a set of patient data to every medic in the world, they'll all tell you the same thing. How the patient presents, how it looks and feels to run that call, which protocol to follow. Once treatment begins, what happens and why can be understood only by the two people crouching over the patient, because each call occupies its own unique space and time. Often the tiniest of details makes the biggest difference. Subtleties are difficult to explain in short answers to pointed questions. Anyway, nobody wants them. The plaintiff's lawyer wants an admission of guilt. The hospital's lawyer wants me to testify that on this call and all the thousands I ran before and the thousands I'll run after, I'm mindlessly following the unimpeachable guidance of a distant, unseen, but all-knowing physician.

I can't satisfy either.

And then, just like that, it's over. Another letter arrives. This one says there's no more case. What happened to it, I don't know. It's dissolved, and nothing further will be required of me.

I'm both relieved and frustrated. True, I've slipped the grip of forces beyond my control, but I've also been left without the opportunity to explain myself or defend myself, to speak to the accusations made against us. My old partner and I are abandoned in a battlefield that suddenly isn't.

And there's nothing positive I can take from the experience.

38

Full Circle

A man falls from a tree. There's nothing dramatic or poetic in the fall, just a jerk as his harness fails and he drops to the ground forty feet below. It's late afternoon, midsummer, hell-hot and Deep South–humid. A second ago he was cutting a dead tree on a forgotten hillside in a land thousands of miles and several countries removed from his own, and now he's broken on the ground. He has no insurance or legal standing, no comprehension of English. The ground below him slopes steeply—a pitiful, weed-choked ravine—which probably saves him but will make rescue no easier. Though his harness fails, his chain saw doesn't, and when he lands, the saw meets his face, cutting a jagged smile from one ear to the next. Skin, meat, sinewy jaw muscles, teeth, tongue, the bones of the jaw itself are all churned up and left to dangle in a horrible and horrifying slurry of mouth parts.

We arrive, park, and tumble down the hill. My partner and the four-man fire crew, fearful of snakes, pick through the weeds with the deliberate caution of soldiers in a minefield. But me? For a moment I'm not there; the weeds, the hill, the almost certain proximity to nervous copperheads, none of it exists. Instead I'm back in July 1997—or, rather, its shadow—and I'm floating in fifty feet of water off a small island not far from Charleston as a member of my tour group coughs his face into the bay. Then my thoughts shift, and I'm sitting in a chair on my first night of tech school. I'm staring at graphic depictions in the back of my brand-new EMT book and wondering if I can do this—*really* do it.

I'm lost in the self-doubt and crushing failures of my past right up until we reach the patient. When we do, I'm abruptly, irrevocably *here*. The world is gone, fallen off without warning, and we've dropped forty feet. There's nothing but massive oral trauma. No one else to turn to, no one to come and shepherd my patient into more capable hands. The call I feared all those years ago has come knocking, and there's nothing to do but run it.

I reach for the suction.

You wouldn't think a single mouth contains so many teeth until they're knocked loose and sent running for cover. The tongue—always in the way—once sliced in half, has an evil twin. There's more blood than you could possibly imagine. We strap him to a backboard and begin the steep climb back up the hill but stop every few feet to set him down and suction out the blood. There's just so much of it. And he's talking, I think, or not. Could be garbled Spanish, could be a gurgle. He's on the stretcher, in the ambulance, in motion.

Oxygen. Then more suctioning, more suctioning. I roll the entire backboard to the left because I can't keep up with the flow. Then he's not talking, not gurgling, nothing. I roll him back and he reanimates. The blood again. More suction. There are teeth on the floor of the ambulance. And then we're there. Through the doors and past triage, a nurse calling from behind us that he's headed to Trauma Two. Surgeons are waiting. They take one look and it's off. Off to another floor, to an OR suite, to a place where they can sort out the pieces and begin the long job of reconstructing a deconstructed face.

By then I'm already gone. Talking to an ER tech named Errol about basketball, about Lebron, about everything but the call. It doesn't occur to me until later that I finally ran the one call I never wanted to run, that the panic I felt all those years ago was the panic of someone else and the person here now simply did his job. Things occasionally come full circle. Sometimes a question posed in the beginning gets answered in the end. And so there it is—a call, The Call, came in, and I showed up. No panic, no mistakes, no doubt. Just me in the ambulance with a horribly mangled face.

I'm tempted to call it perfect.

39

Long Way Gone

At only six weeks, my son gets sick. What started as a fever turns to pneumonia, to a stay in the ICU. He heals, because that's what kids do, but his lungs aren't the same. He's sick again in July, then in August, and after a few months of hope, he's knocked flat in the first few days of November. His pulmonologist suggests we pull him from daycare. I switch to part-time, and like that, I'm no longer a full-time paramedic. The decision is so easy, so obvious, so incidental, it's almost like it never happened. One day I wake up and I'm a stay-at-home dad who happens to ride an ambulance a few nights a week.

I pick up only night shifts, which means getting home at five A.M., catching an hour of sleep, and then being up and on the move with a nine-month-old. Every week I work different days and slightly different hours, and the variation brings forgotten people back into my life. As I run into old partners and friends, I realize that the once new are now seasoned, and many of the once good are now burned out. For a while it's a return to the old days, when everything was new and fun and I couldn't wait to get in. But there's a difference between *being* new and *feeling* new. The excitement fades.

In December 2011 we find out Sabrina is pregnant, and by

August there's a second child in the house. Now I've got two kids at home on an hour's sleep. I cut my nights back from three a week to two. Occasionally, I work one.

Early on in EMT school, my instructor told us that nerves were to be expected—that when a bad call came in, we should expect some excitement and maybe a little dread, and that while we were on-scene and in the ambulance and afterward, when the patient was no longer in our care, we should expect the adrenaline, the fast heart rate, the hyper-focus. That feeling, he said, was what would keep us from making mistakes; it would keep us zeroed in. When it went, we should, too.

That feeling probably left me a while ago, but I don't realize it until I'm kneeling on a balcony outside a second-floor apartment. We're in a crappy part of town, a place I've visited a million times for a million different reasons, some valid. It's somewhere around midnight, perfectly clear, with the kind of gentle temperature that I've come to associate with crazy nights. It's the kind of night I used to love, the kind of call I used to love, but tonight something strange happens—I yawn. The patient is in her fifties, and she was caught in bed with the wrong man and beaten with a bat. The assailant was her daughter, the man was her son-in-law. There are cops everywhere, neighbors surge forward against the loosely strung police tape, and a helicopter churns the air as it sweeps a searchlight over the woods. Blood has been splattered on the walls and pools on the ground, people scream, and a single roll of cotton bandaging that fell from our bag has gotten snared on the handrail and flutters in the breeze. The bat is at my feet.

It's all chaos and madness and the threat of violence from a restless crowd. There are cops and news crews and a genuinely critical patient. Yet I can scarcely muster the energy to care. There's no adrenaline, no hyper-focus. I'm merely an experienced tradesman doing his job. I run the call, finish the shift, clean my ambulance, and punch out.

Sabrina is in the kitchen when I wake up. I walk downstairs. She smiles and asks how my day was.

"I think it's time to quit."

She nods like she's seen this coming all along.

It's impossible to have a serious discussion with kids in the house, so Sabrina and I load them in the car and drive around the city.

"I think this is the right call," Sabrina says about my decision to quit.

I'm not sure what I expected—pushback, maybe, or some frustration—but I definitely didn't expect this. I thought she'd ask what I would do for a job, to make money and contribute. For years she's kept us going. Yes, she balances the checkbook and pays the bills; even all those overdraft fees I incur on my ATM card come down to her. But more than that, she actually *pays* the bills—our money but her salary. I do not live like a normal paramedic. My house, my vacations, my car, my love of lobster, nearly all have come from Sabrina. Half her coworkers think she's a sucker. The other half seem jealous—does *anyone* grow up wanting to work in an office? She has carried our weight for so long that I can't imagine her agreeing to my doing less.

But she sees it differently. All this time, she's been alone.

For years now, during my workweek, we've been ships passing in the night, our interactions reduced to handwritten notes—at once sarcastic and quotidian—scribbled on a pad and left on the counter. Each one is equal parts to-do list, love letter, and death threat: a conjugal visit in imperfect cursive.

Please run the dishwasher if you're going to leave it full.

Would you like a fat lip with that mouth?

Feeling confident?

Maybe. I miss you.

I don't blame you, I'm a lot of fun.

Screw you.

Love you.

You, too.

Most times she doesn't know what I'm doing and is left to guess, drawing on a mental grab bag of all the calls I've run and found strange enough or scary enough to tell her about. Like the time a dispatcher came over the radio to say we'd passed the address and we responded by saying we knew but that they were still shooting, so if she could ask the caller to put down his gun, we'd be glad to go back. And then there are all the domestics we walk into and angry meth heads we fight. The bad neighborhoods, the abandoned buildings, the stray bullets and dirty needles, the perps lurking in the shadows, the horrendous things we see and laugh about but that must be leaving a mark somewhere.

Her phone rang one day: I was on the other line, telling her to turn on the TV. We were supposed to be leaving for Charleston in a few minutes, but there I was, or at least there was my presence, on television at the courthouse downtown. A judge was shot and so was a sheriff, maybe two. Someone was attacked in the parking deck and the shooter—still armed, still creating victims—was out there, too.

We might be a little late to the wedding, guys. Yup. Hazzy's job again.

Our friend Jim has been Sabrina's official stand-in for all dinners, movies, parties, and nights out that I miss. She'd be out having fun, having drinks, having a life, but never far from the understanding that I was out there somewhere—in the middle of a bad neighborhood, a bad call, a bad night. She spent every holiday with someone else. One New Year's Eve, after the toast but before Dick Clark signed off, I called to say I'd just run a bad call. A couple of bodies, one disemboweled, organs in the street. She could hear in my voice that it bothered me, but she was a million miles away, and there was nothing she could do. I told her to call me at midnight, and she said, "It's almost one."

"Oh," I said. "Well, happy New Year."

Driving down the street, with Atlanta slowly rolling past our windows, she says that recently, she's been alone in other ways.

Yes, she thought it was creepy that I cut obits out of the newspaper and keep them in a folder, but for a long time she thought I hadn't changed in any elemental fashion. I'd always considered myself invincible, she says, though not because I'm brave. In her view, I'm full of unearned confidence and possessed of a dreamer's inability to dwell on the past. Death and dead people, the ever-present threat of folding under pressure, she didn't think they affected me.

"You were having too much fun," she says. "You were, I don't know, like an adolescent in search of adventure."

This sounds like the truth.

She didn't expect me to take to the medicine the way I did, but what really surprised her was the way I took to the patients. "Remember Jane?"

I laugh. Jane was a homeless woman, a crack whore, and a regular. Sabrina and I bumped into her one day while we were tailgating a Georgia Tech game and she was digging in the trash. Jane walked right up to me like we were old friends, even knew my wife's name.

"I could tell by the way she looked at you," Sabrina says, "that you treated her with respect. You have a lot of good in you, and this job brought it out."

We ride for a minute in silence, and she's polite enough not to mention Ponytail, Jane's boyfriend, who was also at the game. In what has become a legendary story among our friends, Ponytail nodded to Sabrina and said, "Holla at me, 'cause with an ass like that, I can make you some real money."

After a minute, Sabrina says that something has changed. It's been a while since I've looked forward to work, but I no longer enjoy the patients. I'm gone nights and weekends and most holidays, and when I return, I refuse to talk about it. If I met Jane today, would I still be kind to her? There's no easy answer to that question, because what was once in me is gone. Not gone forever, probably, but gone until I break free. In the meantime, I'm somewhere else, and Sabrina is alone.

I've never thought of it like that before. I was simply a guy pursuing life's darker edges. It never occurred to me that I wasn't making the journey alone, that Sabrina was there the whole time and it was her fight, too. Our marriage has survived a career that breaks so many others because of a lack of secrets—mostly mine—but now Sabrina has laid hers bare.

It's been a long decade for both of us. It's time to come home.

"I think it's time to quit," she says.

I nod like I've seen this coming all along.

•   •   •

By chance, after I turn in my notice, I've got six days off. That's a lot of time to think, to wonder about what I've done and whether, after everything, it's time to go. The decision feels all wrong until I show up the next week. The smell of the ambulance, the scratch of a freshly pressed uniform, the clunk of the boots, all tell me my time has come. Grady is in the midst of a major overhaul—staff, philosophy, everything. They've even changed the uniform. The light blue shirts of my day are gone, and in their place is a gray shirt with black pants. It doesn't look like a Grady uniform. All new employees have been issued the gray, and as existing employees have their annual review, they're given the new color. One by one the old blue disappears. I'm the last holdout. I want to ride out my final days in faded blue.

It isn't just the uniform that makes me stand out. Of Grady's two-hundred-plus employees, I'm one of the ten most senior medics on staff. That's hard to even say. When I started at Grady, I was probably the least experienced medic on the streets. Nearly all of the people I knew and worked with when I started are gone—to other services, to nursing, to med school, to other fields. None of my longtime partners are here. One got hurt, two have been fired, and one quit. The people I looked up to are also gone. A few are supervisors now, the rest scattered in the wind. In the early days of Grady, Atlanta was a city on fire, and it took a different breed to work EMS. When I arrived, most of that first generation was gone, but their acolytes remained, and they passed down their style and approach to the rest of us.

By contrast, those beginning their career now have it a little easier. They're serving a gentrified city and have never known the projects, all of which have been torn down. They don't know the old ambulances or a life before our location was tracked by GPS.

They've been hired by a hospital whose CEO refers to patients as *customers,* and they work out of a new building that doesn't oblige them to walk past Grady's lunatics on the way to a shift. By the time they arrived, we'd gotten our own fuel tanks, so they'll never know what it's like to drive an ambulance on stolen gas. I'm sure they're good, but they're brand-new, mostly, so they don't know—yet—when and how to bend the rules.

In the end, I'm alone. I'm older than most of the new guys, more experienced and angrier, yes, but also more relaxed, more likely to smile when everything goes wrong, because I understand that sometimes things go wrong. Still, when I look around, I don't see familiar faces. I see people who are young and eager and learning, doing all the things I did a decade ago with people who are long gone. I've become a relic.

I work the first two of my final three shifts with a guy just starting his career. My last week is his first. He's twenty-three and clean-shaven. His boots are new. One of the first calls we run together is a bad asthmatic, always my favorite because it's one of the truly life-threatening emergencies we can take from near-death to rebirth all on our own. There are a thousand tricks I've learned through experience, some common to medicine, some unique to a moving vehicle. Everything my rookie does is by the book, which is to say right on paper but wrong for the patient. People who can't breathe feel an animal desire to have their feet on the ground, so I show him how to transport a patient sideways. I show him how to run the steroids through a drip, as opposed to slamming them directly into an IV, because slamming them causes the crotch to burn. I show him how to refill a nebulizer without disconnecting the oxygen. I tell him which questions to ask and how to ask them. I show him everything I know.

When the patient is breathing and able to talk, he nods to the new guy and tells him to listen to me because I know what I'm talking about. That can be said for a lot of people—really, any of the experienced medics we have—but what makes me unique is that I'm about to walk away. In a few days, all that knowledge will get locked away and, slowly, one piece at a time, disappear. From that moment on, I talk incessantly. I'm not sure how much he retains, but I've learned a lot over the years, and for it to simply vanish seems a waste. He's skeptical, I can tell—the new ones always are—but whatever he keeps will serve him. I know that because I, too, was once brand-new and half-lost.

My last shift ended at five A.M. When we got back to Grady, I cleaned the ambulance and made sure it was restocked and ready for the next crew. Nobody was around when I went inside. There was no one to talk to, to say goodbye to, to notice I was leaving. I glanced around at the ambulances, the equipment, caught the smell of disinfectant, the low rumble of a diesel engine, all the things that had been such a part of my life but now weren't, and I clocked out. By the time I got home, I couldn't remember a single call that I'd run that night.

In the end, I wasn't fired. I never fucked up and got drummed out or got angry and stomped off. I never got hurt and ended up in a lingering worker's comp suit, never got promoted up and out of the ambulance. I never even really quit. I went from full-time to part-time to sometimes. My departure went unnoticed and unheralded. In the end, I didn't die—I just faded away.

Epilogue

It's over now.

The ambulance, the partners, the patients, the madness—it's all just a memory. So much has changed, and yet here I am, right back at the beginning. People who meet me now, who didn't know me as a medic, ask what it was like. They ask how many times I've seen the dead, how many children I've delivered. They want to know if I ever threw up or got scared or panicked. They ask about the worst thing I saw and whether it was hard to treat kids. They ask how I got into it. They ask everything, but never once why I stayed. It's as if that original decision to join explained why, a decade later, I was still hanging around. But it didn't. Whatever I thought way back in the beginning, whatever it was that got me hooked, those plans, those hopes, those romantic ideals, didn't survive. Righteous as they might have been, true as they might have been, they couldn't outlast the reality of life on an ambulance: the hours, the pay, the constant threat of injury, the shitholes and the shitbags and the fact that no one not wearing that uniform will ever understand what it is we do.

In the beginning, it was all sirens and heroes and saving lives. A few years later, I hated the sound of sirens. I'd saved lives but never enough, and I'd done heroic things, though never once did I feel like a hero. So why stay?

From that very first night of EMT school, through every shift I ever ran, all the way to the end and as I think back on it now, the question has always been the same: *Why am I here?* It's a complicated question with a simple answer, though it took quitting and walking away before I could see it. People said I'd miss it when I left, that there'd be a hole, a void, hard to describe and harder to fill. They said I'd feel it every day, that quite possibly I'd drift back. There was reason to believe. I've seen plenty of people with no plan B—people raised in an ambulance who knew nothing else—get burned out and leave, only to come back to the one place they've ever felt at home.

Those who return are labeled retreads. Asked to explain why they're back, they'd say it was because they missed the medicine: the IVs and the drugs, the competence, and the unquestioned confidence they earned through years of experience that did them no good anywhere else. Turns out in the real world, you don't get to snake a breathing tube down a dying woman's throat. When you have a regular job, no one gets shot dead in the clay or has back-to-back seizures in the county jail. No one hands you their limp child and places not only their trust but their entire world in your hands. Which is too bad. There's a strange exhilaration not just in having done those things and done them well but in knowing that eventually you'll be called on to do them again.

Still, that's not what I miss. Frankly, I'm not sure that's what anyone misses. Yes, the medicine is the draw, but it's not the show. Everyone who sticks around and anyone who's ever left and considered a comeback knows that there are better places—and better money—in almost any other aspect of the medical field. So why stay? Because the modern world is orderly and practical. The sun goes up, the sun goes down, bills are due, the carpool line starts over there. But it's not so for everyone, and once I realized that, it was hard to walk away. Today, not far from where I'm sitting, the universe will slip a gear and all hell will break loose. Somewhere there's an ambulance crew who knows it. And they're waiting.

So yes, the medicine is great, but you can keep it. I miss the madness. I miss being out at night, running through streets alive with the dead and dying, the drunk, the crazy, the angry, those in need, and those who only think they are. I miss the distant pop of a pistol and the long fading howl of a dealer who's spotted a cop. I miss fighting meth heads in seedy motels, I miss the crack houses and flophouses, the chaos of a shooting scene. I miss the projects after dark. I miss the sense of duty, of honor, of humor, the sense of having lost myself somewhere, somehow, in a very strange world. I even miss the fear of mistakes. Whatever it was that brought us here, it's everything else that kept us around.

People like to say it takes a certain type of person to do this job, a special person. They're probably right, just not in the way they think. Medics don't have to be heroic or tough or even good people. They simply have to enjoy the madness. The normal reaction to gunshots or screaming or house fires or someone collapsing in a messy heap is to get away, to back off, not necessarily to ignore it, perhaps, but not to stumble in half-cocked. And really—aside from a driver's license and a high school diploma—that's what this job takes. A willingness to walk in unprotected when we clearly should walk away. A desire to take part but just as often to bear witness.

So why are medics here? Because panic and death, near death, even your own, is a peculiar drug, and whether or not it's what the injured and the sick and the desperate want to hear, the people who show up do so because they like it. Disasters, even the small ones, mean freedom. Freedom to bend the rules, break the rules, disregard the rules. Maybe I don't even know the rules, just make them up as I go along. The people who stay are the ones who like those moments and all that comes with them, even the hard parts.

Someday it'll be my turn. A call will be placed, an alarm will sound, an ambulance will shudder to life. Six minutes later, weather and distance permitting, two medics will walk through my door. Experience has taught me what they'll find, how they'll react, the things they'll consider when deciding whether or not to save me. That much, at least, is preordained.

And this crew, the one who shows up for my death, will be there for the same reason I hoped to show up for yours.

Because it's fun.

Acknowledgments

To Pepe—for correctly choosing my room out of 250; for convincing me that I could actually make a living as a writer; for believing in me and insisting that I quit my job and start over; for getting nervous but not angry when I got us lost in China; for continuing the fight in 2010 by having our beautiful family; for being there and leading the way; and for having unshakable faith in a man whom the world hadn't yet deemed worthy. It's not enough to say thank you, but there you have it. I love you.

I owe a great debt to Alice Martell. You believed in this book from the moment it came through your door, and you've provided nothing but support and clear guidance. You made this dream a reality. And to Rick Horgan, who understood what I was trying to do from the start. This would not be the book it is without your expert help.

Dan and Jon, who loved the madness as much as I did, and Ciaravella, who encouraged me to write it all down: I'm obliged. To the rest of my EMS family, I consider it a great honor to have served alongside you. Over the years, I routinely found myself, despite the blood and the screaming—and the foul odors—in awe of your courage and dedication. Be safe.

About the Author

Kevin Hazzard served as a paramedic in Atlanta for ten years. Since graduating from The Citadel, he's also worked as both reporter and paperboy. He lives in Manhattan Beach, California, with his wife and their two children, where he writes for television. This is his second book.